In this unique volume, the International Institute for Research and Education's current and previous co-directors explain its origins, activity and challenges.

On 11 June 1981, the Institut international de recherches et de formation pour promouvoir le socialisme scientifique et democratique (later shortened to the more versatile Institut International de Recherche et de Formation) was founded by a Belgian royal charter. It fulfilled a plan by Jacob Moneta, the editor-in-chief of the important big German trade union journal *Metall*, the Belgian Marxist economist Ernest Mandel, the Swiss economist Charles-André Udry and the philologist Jan Philipp Reemtsma. The following summer, the IIRE opened in Amsterdam as a centre for education and research in the service of progressive activists, linked closely to the Marxist and workers' movements worldwide.

After three decades, hundreds of successful seminars, schools and lectures have taken part at the IIRE, with many dozens of participants from every continent the IIRE. In Amsterdam, as in the new IIREs in Manila and Islamabad, its meeting rooms and bedrooms are used by a wide range of progressive activists and organisations. The IIRE is also the home for projects like the *Notebooks for Study and Research*, the Ernest Mandel Study Centre and the Institute for Critical Research.

Figure 1: Some of the attendees at the 2002 LGBT seminar

Figure 2: The IIRE's first director, Pierre Rousset

Living our Internationalism

Figure 3: Ernest Mandel

About the Notebooks for Study and Research

The Notebooks for Study and Research are published by the International Institute for Research and Education. The Notebooks focus on themes of contemporary debate or historical or theoretical importance. Lectures and study materials given in sessions in our Institute, located in Amsterdam, Manila and Islamabad, are made available to the public in large part through the Notebooks.

Since 1986 we have published 50 issues in English. From 1998 they have been published as a book series in collaboration with publishers in London. For many years we had a parallel series in French, the *Cahiers d'étude et de recherche* (currently under review). Different issues of the Notebooks have also appeared in languages besides English and French, including German, Dutch, Arabic, Spanish, Japanese, Korean, Portuguese, Turkish, Swedish Danish and Russian.

Figure 4: Livio Maitan (1923-2004), one of the IIRE's most popular lecturers, wrote a Notebook for Study and Research on Italian communism

Living our Internationalism

The first thirty years of the International Institute for Research & Education

Edited by Joost Kircz and Murray Smith
Preface by Marijke Colle

With contributions from Susan Caldwell, Antonio Carmona Báez, Heather Dashner, Peter Drucker, Penelope Duggan, Pierre Rousset, Sally Rousset and Bertil Videt

International Institute for Research & Education, Amsterdam
Resistance Books, London

Both the International Institute for Research and Education and Resistance would be glad to have readers' opinions of this book, its design and translations, and any suggestions you may have for future publications or wider distribution.

Our books are available at special quantity discounts to educational and non-profit organizations, and to bookstores.

To contact us, write to: Socialist Resistance, PO Box 62732 London SW2 9GQ, email contact@socialistresistance.org or visit: www.socialistresistance.org

Published by Resistance Books, December 2010

Printed in Britain by Lightning Source

ISBN 978-0-902869-83-7

© International Institute for Research and Education, 2010.

Published as issue 41 of the *Notebooks for Study and Research*.

ISSN 0298-7902

Designer : Claude Roelens-Dequidt

Figure 5 Stèphanie Treillet (at the centre,) who gives economic lectures for the IIRE, at the 2003 Global Justice school

Contents

Figure 6: Charles-André Udry

Preface: Three decades of open and non-dogmatic Marxism.
Marijke Colle

The strength of the IIRE remains its commitment to an open and non-dogmatic Marxism that is not sectarian and reflects the realities of the changes in the world.

This book describes how a fantastic project dreamed up by a group of dedicated revolutionary Marxists was put in place and how, guided by their political experience and their theoretical background, a unique school became reality.

From three-month education sessions for full time cadres of the sections of the workers' movement in the eighties, to the incorporation of new themes and new forms of action in the anti-globalisation movement worldwide in the nineties, we are now witnessing the modular three weeks of the Global Justice Schools in Amsterdam, and the establishment of an IIRE in Manila and an IIRE in Islamabad.

There are practical reasons for these changes in the educational and theoretical activities of the IIRE, but of course, those are also the result of worldwide political changes since the 1980s.

As Pierre Rousset writes in this book, after the experiences of the seventies, *"we went through a fundamental re-examination of a whole series of questions, such as the definition of a strategy or the concept of 'revolutionary subject' and how to articulate struggle and emancipation, struggles against oppression and the class struggle."*

The strategic discussion, the reframing of 'old beliefs' in the context of the new realities of concrete party building by a new generation, emerging after 1968 worldwide, gave us the very rich materials for the first series of Notebooks produced by the IIRE.[1]

"Through much of the 1990s, intellectual renewal at the IIRE took place in something of a vacuum, in the context of social movements and a radical left that were shrinking and on the defensive. By the end of the decade, though the challenges facing the left remained daunting, debates at the institute were more and more responses to questions being posed in revitalized movements and parties."(Peter Drucker)

When the immediate possibility of revolutions receded during the difficult period of the nineties and we witnessed the global neo-liberal offensive and the collapse of the Stalinist states, the emphasis

---

1   The Notebooks are listed on pages 102-104.

of the schools changed. New themes, new actions, new international networks emerged and enriched our world view. The anti-globalisation movement gave us a first glimmer of hope, despite its lack of theoretical and organisational structures. The movement built its own dynamics and formulated its own truly worldwide radical criticism of capitalism.

The last period witnessed a radical renewal, physically (our new premises), geographically (a new neighbourhood in Amsterdam) and worldwide (IIRE in Manila and in Islamabad).

In my view, the necessity of getting the IIRE on the web was in part due to the new development of the World Social Forum processes – and other international progressive responses – that used the web to organise, coordinate and distribute a political understanding that 'there is an alternative'. (Susan Caldwell)

Today there is a real new network of IIREs in the making.

As travel costs and a lack of possibilities to take time of from work make participation in the schools organized by the IIRE in Amsterdam more difficult, we must look for alternatives and use the new technologies to the full.

The development and diversification of internet tools offers radical new possibilities for reaching out and discussing with more people than ever. We are consolidating internet conferences with staff in Manila and Islamabad. MP3 files of our lectures are increasingly being used by young (and not so young) people.

Establishing two new Institutes, one in Manila and one is Islamabad is a major step forward and reflects important political developments in Asia.

The IIRE in Amsterdam, in Manila and in Islamabad, are not part of a uniform worldwide brand comparable to a McDonalds chain or to Stalinist international organisations. On the contrary, each institute aims at serving its own regional needs in the first place.

The first two successful Global Justice Schools held in Manila in 2009 and 2010 show that IIRE-Manila is already working as a catalyst for the strengthening of the radical left in South-East Asia and for the organisation of seminars to analyse more in depth the changes that are taking place in that region of the world.

The first Global Justice School in Islamabad, Pakistan (October 2010) held under extremely difficult circumstances, after the terrible floods and in a country at war, demonstrates that a dynamic political organisation can offer even in those difficult circumstances, important educational activities to its local cadres.

In its current Amsterdam setting, the IIRE is confronted with the challenge of combining commercial activities with the organisation of schools and seminars.

The IIRE Amsterdam continues to organize its three week Global Justice Schools aimed not only at members of the workers' movement but also in collaboration with the CADTM network and inviting activists who are keen on reflecting and elaborating in a collective way, the analyses and the strategies necessary in our common anti-capitalist struggles.

IIRE Amsterdam also continues with the organisation of thematic seminars and has plans for new publications.

We hope that this endeavour will contribute to the building of a new radically anti-capitalist global framework incorporating new problems (ecology, Islamophobia, the rise of the populist extreme right parties in Europe, the deep economic crisis and its repercussions) and building a strong global resistance to the crisis.

This is the only way in which 'another world can become possible'.

Enjoy reading this testimony of the reality of radical politics in the last quarter of the 20th century and the start of the 21st century!

Figure 7: CADTM founder, and IIRE Fellow, Eric Toussant

Introduction: Looking back and setting a new stage for the IIRE.
Joost Kircz

On its 25th anniversary the International Institute for Research and Education was going through a real metamorphosis. We did not only leave our old building in order to start with a clean slate in new and beautiful premises, with the most up-to-date technical and construction features. Our whole way of operating changed: from now on we aim to operate as a professional conference centre and concentrate more on our role in centralising the development of socialist theory and furthering strategic political debates on the left.

As Marxists, we take the historical record very seriously. We want to learn from our experiences and expand our continuing interactions with political activists and scholars, old and young, in order to develop our activities in tune with the beat of time.

After our 25th anniversary and the official opening of our new headquarters, we asked our activists who were instrumental in reaching the present stage to write down their personal memoirs and reflections. In the next pages you will find contributions from those who were able, in the short time allowed them, to contribute. It goes without saying that this is a dynamic document, inasmuch as reflections and memoirs will always be augmented by others and deepened in content in the course of the permanent discussions that take place at the IIRE.

Below I will sketch a short overall history, hopefully giving due credit to all those people who were central in building the IIRE. This is not the place to dwell further on the interesting theme of the role of the individual in history. It is clear to everybody that a collective project like ours is dependent on the hundreds of participants who visited us and participated in courses, sessions and meetings. However, in this ever changing stream of enthusiastic people, some names stand out.

As explained in the contribution of our first programme director Pierre Rousset and Sally Rousset, the political scene in the 1970s was very different from today. In that period, in which the outlook for socialist-oriented developments was considered as much more positive then now, the overall need for the development of political answers firmly grounded in Marxism was felt everywhere. With hindsight, we can say that objectively that need only kept growing in the later downturn.

It was in those enthusiastic years that an excellent idea could merge with a unique occasion. A close German sympathiser, Jan Philipp Reemtsma, inherited a serious amount of capital from his industrialist father. With a sharp eye for Germany's terrible record in the Second World War, he decided wisely that this money must become an investment in the study for a better world. In close collaboration with his political friends and teachers, in particular Jacob Moneta, the editor-in-chief of the important big German trade union journal *Metall*, the Belgian Marxist economist Ernest Mandel and the Swiss economist Charles-André Udry, the idea of an international intellectual centre was coined. Taking as reference points the famous Comintern party school in Berlin in the early 20s and the Frankfurt School in the 30s, it was felt that the time was ripe to join forces and bring together cadres and young activists to recreate a real research and education centre for the development of emancipatory ideas and socialist theory.

Due to the solid work of the Belgian lawyer Nathan Weinstock, author of the famous book *Le sionisme contre Israel* ("Zionism, False Messiah" in the English translation), a Belgian international scientific association was established, called: *Institut international de recherches et de formation pour promouvoir le socialisme scientifique et democratique*. This institute was not created as one of the many non-profitmaking foundations we see everywhere. No, the institute obtained special and fairly unique official royal recognition as an accepted international association. As Brussels is the base for many international institutions, we share this status with one of our archenemies, NATO. On 11 June 1981, the official papers in the name of the Belgian King Boudewijn (Baudouin) were stamped. It goes without saying that this status helped us a lot in the years to come. The association has members and an executive board.

In the good spirit of Leninist (and Mandelist) revolutionary voluntarism, a series of initiatives quickly developed. There were ideas for major international conferences, for a programme of stipends for left wing scholars to write books and the establishment of the Amsterdam Institute as the headquarters and material incarnation of all our plans. The institute, which quickly adopted the name IIRF (IIRE in English), since the imposing long title was hardly practical for daily usage, received a considerable sum of money to help it get off the ground, enabling us to buy and renovate a building.

In Germany, Reemtsma founded in 1984 the Hamburger Institut für Sozialforschung, a research foundation fostering mainly sociological and historical research, which still plays an important role with advanced studies and publications in a broader democratic and emancipatory context.[2]

Unfortunately, the way the two initiatives worked out in daily practice led to a divide and ultimately to a divorce.

As soon as the IIRF was established Ernest Mandel and Charles-André Udry contacted brokers in order to find a pleasant, safe and solid building in which to establish a real institute. With the help of the Swiss architect, François Iselin, a building was found in Amsterdam and François signed for the first sketch plans. Amsterdam was chosen because in that period the Netherlands was one of the most open and hospitable countries, whereas Belgium had a much more repressive regime towards foreigners. After a series of attempts, finally four old houses in Willemparkweg 202-208, close to the famous Vondelpark in the rich southern part of the city, were found and acquired in December 1981. From that moment, Dutch labour was called in. I was invited to join the board as project manager and immediately learned the hard way the difference between excellent plans and the way society operates, in the form of regulations, laws and bureaucracy. At the same time Robert Went and his companion Elsa van der Heijden joined the project team and moved from Leiden to Amsterdam to start camping in the empty building in order to safeguard it. This was the beginning of Robert's career shift from handyman to becoming an economist.

As Dutch soil is much weaker than Swiss rock and the building regulations very much different, the local architect Willem Vermeer and his team were hired. Willem was a most talented craftsman, who not only looked after the architectural aspects but acted as a contractor at the same time. An additional advantage was that he was extremely communicative, kept all his administration open for inspection any time and had a keen eye for renovation projects and a deep attachment to "underlayment" (also called multiplex[3]) which was used throughout the building. Unfortunately Willem passed away a few years ago. With enormous enthusiasm, the building was renovated, and many a left-wing craftsman and woman in Amsterdam can remember the team spirit and the high pace of work, while the day frequently ended with a huge meal in Willem's office.

When in June 1982 a large Milanese lorry unloaded a unique, and very cheap, collection of design furniture, the institute could open its doors. Many a visitor will look back with mixed feelings on the orange and blue chairs, which are nowadays considered as pieces

---

2   http://www.his-online.de
3   In less technical language, plywood

of art, which means to look at, not to sit on. With a good sense of historical continuity, our new chairs are also of Italian make.

After rearranging the four buildings into housing space, consisting of three flats in one house and one big institute in the other three, it became possible to start operations. Robert and Elsa lived in the ground floor apartment, which was equipped with a door leading directly into the reception area of the institute. Pierre and his companion Sally Rousset, got the 2nd floor, which had its own entrance, whilst the 3rd floor was used by our first co-director along with Pierre, the Belgian François Vercammen.

François stayed until 1985, which was only a relatively short time, certainly compared to Pierre, Robert and later Peter. From that time the 3rd floor was mainly used for regular visitors who stayed over a longer period. François was succeeded by the Amsterdam historian Herman Pieterson, who also stayed on for three years and left in 1988.

During all those years Robert acted as a jack-of-all-trades, but stimulated by the activities of the institute, turned his interest in economics into a part-time university study, which he crowned in 1996 with a dissertation on Globalization. When Herman left, Robert became co-director and stayed almost until the turn of the century. Unfortunately our longest serving friend, who indisputably played the single most important role in keeping the institute alive, could not find time to write a contribution.

When Pierre and Sally returned to Paris, after almost 11 years, Peter Drucker from New York joined us in 1993 and stayed until 2006, closing the doors of the old building. Unfortunately we have to remember that Peter was the last non-EU citizen for whom we could obtain a legal working permit. Peter and Robert as co-directors developed an efficient collaboration. In Peter's contribution you can read what happened in that period. In the same period Robert's publications on globalization made his name as a recognized expert.

When Robert and Elsa left the institute to start living in an independent home of their own, we were finally able to take on a full time female programme director, in the person of Susan Caldwell from Canada. As Susan was on leave from a tenure position in Québec, she could work as a volunteer, though for all the time she was here we tried and failed to get a work permit for her. Susan stayed until 2004, and her souvenirs of her time here are printed below. In 2005 the Franco-Scot Murray Smith joined us as a co-director[4], while on

---

4   After Murray's retirement, Dr Antonio Carmona Báez was co-director in

January 2nd 2007, the Dane Bertil Videt, just back from sociological field work in Eastern Turkey, became co-director for the next years to come.

After having named all the programme directors, it is time to list some of the invaluable collaborators without whom the institute could never have survived. First of all, we have to name Sally Rousset, who as companion of Pierre became one of the pillars of the operation. Not only did she take care of an avalanche of administrative work, she also kept active in Philippine solidarity work and became a stable cornerstone of the institute. Also in the early days, Michèle Vermeulen joined the staff, first as volunteer and later as part-timer, and remained until very recently. Michèle, who outdid even Robert in being always present, played a crucial social role. With her mastery of Dutch, French, English and particularly Spanish, she befriended many visitors and became one of the people who kept the whole machinery rolling. In 1993 Christopher Beck joined Peter in Amsterdam, and became the trusted watch dog of our extensive library, a role he continues to fulfil today. With Eva Ferraren from the Philippines, we have also established a solid and important tie with the large immigrant population in Europe. Eva also participates as a staff member in the organisation of schools, were she also often gives reports. It goes without saying that the list of people who helped us out on many an occasion is very long. We have had regular Basque and Swiss groups who came in the summer to help with interior construction work, repairs and so on. We have seen many people lecturing and spending much time working with our students and visitors. All those people contributed enormously to the well being of the institute. We are very pleased that one of our permanent collaborators from the start, Penelope Duggan, has contributed to this special Notebook.

A new phase

The passing away of Ernest Mandel in 1995 was a great loss to all of us. In particular in the second half of the 90s it became clear that much had to be done in order to keep the institute up and running. Financially the situation became very tight. Political culture declined and donations, our main source of income, dried up. But also the building was aging. Regulations on fire prevention and Legionnaires' Disease, just to name a couple of important issues, demanded major renovations and even major changes in the construction of the building. Also, on the legal and tax front regulations changed. In the same Ernestian

---

2008-2009. Marijke Colle succeeded Antonio.

spirit which created the institute, we took action to pull off the trick again. In recent years our statutes have been adapted to the present day Belgian regulations. We made a clear move to stop the ambiguity of being semi-Belgian, semi-Dutch. We are still a Belgian international association, though we shortened our name to *Institut international de recherches et de forrmation*, a name that at least fits into formal administrative data records. We made a clear choice to have all economic operations only in the Netherlands and are registered here as a research and conference centre. Even our names - IIRF in French, IIRE in English and IIIR in Spanish - are now officially registered.

Figure 8: Joost Kircz puts up the IIRE's door sign from Willemspark-weg on the door of the new Institute

As in capitalist society we have laws, we decided to use them. This enabled us to do a somersault. We were able to sell the old premises for a good price and bought a part of a large renovation project in a working-class neighbourhood in the eastern part of town, which is now in full renovation. This way we not only have a new and completely renovated building which complies with all official laws and regulations, but have also been able to renovate the place according to our needs for the years to come. This time Marian van der Waals is our architect. Only a small band of volunteers and part-timers together with Bertil, Eva and Murray made up the group that converted the IIRF into its new shape. Jakob Wedemeijer, Eng Que, Abel Malek Mellouk, myself and most of all our volunteer removal manager Wim

Seegers who, being a professional documentalist, played the role of organisational linchpin in this ambitious game of socialist turn-around management. In the process of removal and refurnishing the new building we got invaluable help from volunteers from France, the Philippines, Italy and Denmark.

Our rebirth will enable us to develop new vistas and hark back to the original dreams and objectives, to become an open and dynamic study and research centre for democratic and scientific socialist endeavours. Over the past years we have worked very hard and have given the IIRF a thorough renewal. Under our new directorship we will continue our voyage.

Figure 9: The IIRE's volunteer removal team with Murray Smith (with glasses, at end of table), co-director from 2005 to 2008.

1982-1992: IIRE's first decade.
Pierre Rousset & Sally Rousset

The International Institute for Research and Education (IIRE) opened its doors in September 1982, in Amsterdam. Now it has left its venerable premises on Willemsparkweg, where it had become a landmark. The move is a good opportunity to look back on the first decade of a rather unique activist initiative.

At the end of the 1970s, when it was first envisaged, the plan seemed madness: founding an international institute where activists, coming from the five continents[5] and hailing from political currents from different traditions, could spend several months together studying, revisiting the history of the socialist struggle in order to reflect on their own experiences of struggle and the lessons of them. This entailed a significant material investment, starting with a building where some thirty participants in the case of the long sessions (and up to twice as many for short meetings) could live, work and discuss.

Our aim was a very ambitious one, materially and politically — so much so that it may well have seemed above our forces. To our knowledge, it was unprecedented — and remains so to this day. "Red universities" of the past were state initiatives, organised by the USSR, East Germany or China... So they are not at all comparable. In September 1982, when we opened the IIRE to welcome the first international session, we had no idea how long such an experiment could last. We wanted to ensure five years of activities at the least, but we had developed an institute with an aim of lasting far longer. And yet, knowing that the situation in the 1980s was far from favourable, we were careful to avoid making over-optimistic prognoses.

Three decades later, IIRE is still standing. We have even moved into new premises to start off a new life cycle. Over the years, many things have changed, so we would like to take the opportunity to look back at the Institute's first decade, to make sure this slice of history does not fall into oblivion.

The organisations at the heart of the process

Back in 1982 and to this day, IIRE has co-operated with organisations. The national organisations concerned (and not the Institute) chose the participants — who all had activist responsibilities. It was

---

5   This common formula is obviously inaccurate, dividing in two a single continent (Eurasia) and leaving out Antarctica.

organisations which were contacting one another through the Institute.

It was also the organisations, and not the participants alone, who were intended to reap the benefits of the political education, the attempt to develop theory on a common basis and the international exchanges the IIRE made possible. And in turn, the organisations, through their cadres, provided the Amsterdam staff with the benefit of their own experience.

To achieve results, this give-and-take among the national organisations and the IIRE took time. It is very difficult for a single participant, returning home, to communicate what she or he learnt during an international educational session. This transmission became more effective when, in time, ten or twenty cadres had made the trip. In the same vein, by taking part repeatedly in Institute sessions, an organisation can make a far more effective contribution than through one meeting in the evolution of the theoretical work. From year to year, the courses and reports presented at Amsterdam have changed, even when their title has remained the same.

To a large extent, the quality of what was achieved in Amsterdam reflected the wealth of experience of the organisations taking part in the sessions — whether by providing course participants or speakers and staff. The wealth of these experiences, but also, their limits: the efforts at theoretical development that accompanied the educational work and the Institute staff's ability to take the initiative levelled off after the first decade in existence. We'll come back to this in the conclusion.

Of course, the Amsterdam Institute did not merely passively take in the contributions of the national organisations. It had a very important international role in driving things forward. It built a team of staff and facilitators without whom the work of transmitting and collectivising ideas, and taking theoretical work to a deeper level would have been impossible. But the initial choice (to be at the service of the organisations) had many implications. Just to give one example, concerning the makeup of sessions: IIRE always asked the national leaderships to prioritise sending women cadres. Despite this, the percentage of women only reached 30% at most, during the "long" educational sessions. But it would not have been either proper or possible for the Institute to take over the national leaderships' job of choosing participants and ensuring parity.

The composition of the sessions reflected the organisations' and their leadership networks' realities. And obviously there was a very wide range of participants. One "typical" profile was very common, however: activists who came from a rather popular or working-class background, but who had reached university — though often they had never found time to finish their studies. This reality is far different from the stereotype of spoilt wealthy leftist kids the media so often portray. It would be very interesting to compile statistical data on the composition of the sessions of the first years, in order to compare them with subsequent periods.

Originality of the sessions

There are many elements of continuity in IIRE history, including this privileged relationship with organisations and with militant commitment. However, there have also been many changes. The most obvious was the length of the sessions. The Amsterdam Institute's "founding period" was characterised by "long" sessions: two three-month international sessions were organised every year.

These "education" sessions (the quotes are used to show that far more was involved) and the Institute's other activities had to meet several aims:

- To provide activists with an opportunity to get away from daily activism and find the time to read, study and reflect with a clear head. Such time to learn and think was a luxury in many organisations at that time! - To bring together cadres from organisations in different regions of the world, in order to compare continental experiences and overcome language barriers that mean that even within our International, reading matter and references are not the same among English, French and Castilian speakers (not to mention Portuguese speakers or non-Western cultural frameworks).

- To open the Institute up to all radical activist organisations who were interested, and not only the sections of the Trotskyist movement, to lay the groundwork for an exchange among "revolutionary Marxist", "Trotskyist", "Maoist", "Guevarist" and other traditions (the quotes are to remind us how simplistic, or even misleading, such labels can be).

- To combine in a single session education and the development and collective appropriation of ideas. This meant going back over the theoretical foundations of Marxism, as well as the history of the socialist movement and revolutions, but also trying to renew our thinking in the light of the experience of the 1960s and 1970s. This lead us to one of our most original aims during the IIRE's first decade, which we will return to in more detail: cadres who had begun their political activity in the 1960s or early 1970s (the "1968 generation") wanted to use the Institute to draw a kind of mid-way balance sheet, to draw lessons from the first twenty years of their political commitment.

Concretely, the way sessions were organised was a compromise between these aims and our possibilities.

Each session lasted three months and dealt with a wide spectrum of topics; theory, history, strategy, feminism, organisational principles, specific case studies... In terms of such ambitious aims (including time to read) and the scope of the programme, three months was still a very short time. But it was also very long for the participants and their organisations.

Moreover, after two three-month sessions per year (that is seven months on the premises, taking participants' comings and goings into account), there was very little time left to host other types of meetings.

In the light of its international vocation, the Institute functioned in three (Western) languages: English, French and Spanish. But each three-month session only used two at once, otherwise interpreting and communication among participants would have been too complicated.

However, for example in an English/Castilian session, French-speaking organisations were asked to send members who spoke at least one of the other two languages. But activists in that period were not particularly skilled in foreign languages and the geographical composition of the sessions was never as balanced as we would have liked: many Asians in the case of sessions using English, many Latin-Americans in the case of ones using Castilian.

Living there

For three months, around 20 participants[6] lived and worked in the Institute. This meant they needed appropriate meeting and living places. Amsterdam was a major airline hub (easily accessed internationally) and was not too far from the main "organisational support base" that the Amsterdam team relied on (in France) as well as help provided in the Netherlands, and provided a very rich cultural environment: there were many other things to see than the IIRE's activist library! The Institute's own buildings, with their perilous steep staircases that people had to learn to navigate safely, were an invitation to discover the Dutch mentality.[7]

---

6   The number of participants in sessions ranged from 11 to 28.
7   There is a historical materialist explanation for almost everything. The "harshness" of these steep stairs was not the result of Calvinism, but rather, as we have been told, the calculation of the housing tax on the basis of the

These buildings had to be entirely renovated to accommodate the Institute as a place for work and daily life, with an excellent architectural redesign. With, on four storeys: a meeting room that could accommodate sixty people and two smaller ones: two library floors; two storeys accommodating the bedrooms and showers; a large collective kitchen and refectory; apartments for the residential staff team: finally, to relax together, a music room, a TV room and a small garden — not forgetting the vast, green Vondelpark next door, so handy for walking Beno the dog, strolling and relaxing, for athletes to jog, for dreaming and sharing tender moments (or even for the practice of urban ornithology[8])... As months went by, the participants who came from tropical climes got a glimpse of the passing seasons in a temperate zone. We should not underestimate the importance of such places for encounters, inside or outside the premises!

Other than immersing themselves in political study, participants also had to do (large-scale!) shopping and cooking, wash clothes, do the housework and keep the premises clean... They weren't on holiday! Our budgets did not allow us to rely on professional staff, and from an activist standpoint, it may have been better not to. We had to organise cooking teams with at least one person who knew how to cook — and cook on a group scale! The results were honourable, if unequal. Each session lived through a "food war" (was it really necessary to serve turkey at Thanksgiving, and what about other holidays?) (Did cheeses have to be safeguarded against midnight raids?)

More seriously, the 1980s brought the AIDS crisis. Facing up to this new disease took time, at different speeds according to the region, the country or the milieu. As a necessary precautionary principle in an International Institute, for a while we had to emphasise the reality of the risk, during the introductory meeting: "No condom, no fun!" I was perplexed by the glances of certain participants: were they thinking: "who the hell does he think I am? I'm just here to study politics!" Or was it a suspicious look: "Is he a meddling old busybody hiding his moralistic outlook behind spurious health considerations?"

Three months in a small, multicultural community seems like a long time. It means time for study and exchanges, but also for crises, whether personal or more collective, to come to a head. The journey to Amsterdam uprooted more than one participant. Adults found them-

surface area taken up by buildings.

8   See: Rousset, Pierre, 'Notes on Casual Encounters with Amsterdam Vondelpark's Birds' (The Netherlands, 1984-1991), 23 December 1991; and: 'Complementary Notes on Casual Encounters with Amsterdam Vondelpark's Birds' (The Netherlands), 24 December 1992 (photocopies).

selves back at school desks and hyper-activists had to sit and listen quietly. A considerable percentage of the participants —40%— had never travelled outside their home country before attending our educational sessions and found themselves strangers in a strange land. In unfamiliar territory, and an emotional desert, everyday behaviour expressed both each person's psychological makeup and different regional and organisational cultures. In this closed space, gender relations were not always simple, and female under-representation didn't make matters easier. On top of these, the education provided was designed to be critical – and often provided more questions than answers.

In three months' time, crises that generally didn't arise during shorter sessions had time to come to a head. If there were indeed crises, and a small number of these proved serious, they were much less common than we had feared. Because most of the participants were organisational cadres. Because the regular meetings of the women's commission played a very positive role. Because the Institute staff – where everyone played a role, from the central organisers to Michèle – was there to listen.

A range of activities flourished

Although preparing for and holding the three-month sessions took up a good share of the Institute's time and material and human resources, this work also encouraged us to organise a whole series of initiatives. The sessions were the root and trunk of a whole range of activities.

The long sessions made it possible to devote much time to reading. Certain participants came with a firm commitment to finally wade through some weighty tome, such as Capital, for which they had simply never found the time. The speakers also needed reference material on hand. It was a time when former activists were selling off their political books, which we found in second-hand bookshops (proving that every cloud has a silver lining). Over the years, we built up a multilingual library that, at the end of the first decade, numbered approximately twenty thousand volumes and many sets of periodicals.

Reams of photocopied material were handed out to the participants. This literature was recycled afterwards in many national organisations. As the lecture outlines often became more substantial from session to session, we had the raw material to launch two series of publications, the Working papers (for work in progress) and the

Notebooks for Study and Research (NSR). These Notebooks, produced from 1986 onwards, were systematically published in French and in English, to provide a common reference on an international level.

Our resources did not allow us to do more, but certain NSR were translated into Castilian, German, Turkish, Dutch, Swedish, Japanese, Russian and Danish. Twenty-one issues of this series of Notebooks came out by 1993.[9]

Finally, the existence of our premises and the dynamics of the contacts made among facilitators and organisations led to other types of meetings in Amsterdam: thematic seminars or working meetings: on economics, women, ecology, youth... As long as the three-month meetings lasted, there was not much time available for these various meetings.

An international team

IIRE's residential staff has always been very small: four people, and sometimes only three. It carried a particular responsibility for the political continuity and administrative tasks of the Institute. However the staff alone could never have got the job done. A network of facilitators contributed to holding the sessions. These people were not only lecturers, far from it. The main facilitators remained at least 15 days in Amsterdam, so they could discuss informally with the participants and keep a close eye on the debates. They were members of the Fourth International's leadership or of the leadership of national organisations. Their presence was an opportunity for exchanges that went far beyond the scope of their lectures. They were not "guest speakers" presenting a lecture: they took part in a collective political task. In fact, not only were they not paid for their attendance, they paid for their own meals! Even though the cost of meals was modest, even though we had a very tight budget and the symbol was strong, this was perhaps a bit much to ask. But such details illustrate the spirit in which the Institute operated.

---

9   The complete bilingual series of CER/NSR in French and English includes 25 issues. Other than original writings based on the Institute's work, these Notebooks also include texts written on other occasions. Afterwards, the English-language edition, — the Notebooks for Study and Research— continued to come out, but not the French.

The leadership team of the international school involved the permanent staff (the "residents") and the most regular facilitators. This is what made it possible to stand firm and resist a few blows of outrageous fortune. Moreover, holding the sessions would have been impossible without an active network of volunteer translators and interpreters who also spent long periods at the Institute. The simultaneous translation equipment they used was purpose-built by a Swiss inventor activist: high-tech craftwork! The Swiss also developed the architectural redesign. Some national organisations (such as the Basques) even organised working holiday sessions to repaint and freshen up the Institute's lecture halls. It might seem strange to thank all the people who took part in a collective task (for we all took a hand in it) but let's do it anyway: on behalf of the resident staff of the Institute in the 1980s, thanks for the efforts made by the non-residents: cadres, lecturers and interpreters, activists...

Figure 10: Some of the IIRE's volunteer translators, including former co-director Peter Drucker (Top left)

The facilitators came from several continents and many countries. However, for financial reasons above all – we paid their travel costs, which was the least we could do – the geographical representation of the IIRE "facilitator" network remained unequal, with an over-representation of Europe (and particularly France). On the other hand, if this is some compensation, the Third World (Latin America and Asia especially) was often better represented among the students than the Europeans. We did make a very big financial effort to help these participants come to the Institute[10]

10   Of course, Third World organisations paid far less than their counter-

This international network of activist facilitators ran at full speed for several years; many of the members of this international team returned session after session, twice a year. This made it possible not only to ensure the level of the sessions, but also to create a real framework for making our theoretical work a collective effort.

Pooling knowledge and developing ideas

Work on pooling our knowledge became even more important because the Amsterdam Institute opened its doors in the early 1980s, when it became particularly crucial for an activist generation, from the 1960s-1970s, to reflect on their work. They had accumulated a body of work from which it was possible to draw conclusions. After a period of rapid construction of new organisations, this generation faced an often unexpected and problematic change in the political situation, and encountered crises. The IIRE's work played a part in getting through this period. It also created new pressures that forced the facilitators to produce new courses and writings.

Activist cadres rarely have the time to write, and not all have the talent. Of course, more than one member of the IIRE's team of facilitators could list several university degrees. But the essential factor lay elsewhere: in a significant attempt to reflect on the situation, supported by activist experience.[11] This collective theoretical effort was also carried out in other places besides the Amsterdam Institute, but the IIRE did have two rare assets: time, and being able to step back and see in perspective international events that generally weighed down the agendas of other international meetings. So the dialogue on fundamental questions also went on not only among the facilitators, but also with the course participants. More than once, the latter raised incisive questions, forcing the lecturers to revise their notes.

IIRE's original teaching did not depend on pedagogical aids. In that field we were really far from being in the vanguard. Except for the odd video, ill-adapted maps and an underused overhead projector,

parts in "rich" countries, and there was special assistance for the most deprived countries. However, with a very few rare exceptions, each organisation paid something, whether part of its travel and stay costs, or, at the least, the pocket money so its participants could go out in Amsterdam.
11   The academic world often behaves as if it has a monopoly over the production of knowledge. Academics cite one another to justify their theses and treat social movements as "case studies" and their members as "source material". Each has a role to keep to: academics think, political scientists explain, journalists report and activists organise. And yet, as by miracle, the latter also think...

we stuck with the blackboard and photocopies. We did not have the time to learn audiovisual methods (a novelty for us) nor the appropriate computerised material.

During a typical day, the morning was devoted to a lecture (three times three-quarters of an hour), the afternoon to reading, then discussions in commissions or in a general meeting.

Some evenings, the course participants presented the situation in their countries and their organisations' activities.

On the other hand, in terms of content and dynamics, the education provided was original — in more than one respect: Through the dialogue that we encouraged among course participants, facilitators and resident staff, which enabled us to go over fundamental issues in greater depth over a session; Through the way the study of the past (reference texts, revolutions and struggles...) was tied to our own contemporary experience; Through a close relationship established between a systematic return to the "fundamentals" of living Marxism and an equally systematic effort to keep it up to date.

Figure 11 - Livio Maitan (centre) with participants at the IIRE's 2000 North-South School

A focus for reflection

IIRE became a focus for the development of theory. An array of questions was taken up.

During the 1970s, a broad range of struggles developed — from this standpoint, it was a particularly rich period, although this richness is often forgotten, obscured or overlooked these days. Strikes once again took the form of experiments in workers' control. A new feminist generation stormed onto the scene and most of the theoretical renewal, especially in this field, already took place during this decade, with in particular the development of a "class struggle" feminist current. Questions of "everyday life" were seen as political issues.

Education, health, psychiatry, sport and art ... all sectors of social activity were subjected to the test of anti-capitalist criticism.

In the 1970s, revolution also remained a living reality (Nicaragua!). Some solidarity activities had to be conducted in a strictly clandestine way, including towards Eastern European countries (as in the case of Solidarność[12]). Some of our organisations were still clandestine, for example, in Europe, those in the Spanish State and in Greece. And some were even directly involved in armed struggles (Basque Country, Argentina...). But after these years in which "It was the hour of the furnaces, and only the light should be seen..." (José Marti), we had to deal with a changing political situation in Europe (an unexpected "return to normalcy"), with terribly costly errors in human terms in Latin America, with the effects of the Pol Pot regime[13] and the Sino-Indochinese crisis in Asia[14], and increasingly varied "frames of reference" (from the Brazilian Workers' party (PT) to Nicaraguan Sandinism!).[15]

It is no wonder that during the following decade, we went through a fundamental reexamination of a whole series of questions, such as the definition of a strategy or the concept of "revolutionary

12   Solidarity was the first independent trade union in a Warsaw Pact country. In the 1980s it constituted a broad anti-bureaucratic social movement.

13   Prime Minister of Cambodia from 1976–1979, when he attempted to "cleanse" the country, resulting in the deaths of two million people.

14   A brief but bloody border war fought in 1979 between the People's Republic of China (PRC) and Vietnam.

15   On this question of the transition from the 1970s to the 1980s in France (and part of Europe), you will find some elements in: Pierre Rousset, '1965-2005: From the mid-1960s to the Present: Two generations in the evolution of the European Radical Left and some "burning issues"'. Published on the ESSF website: http://bit.ly/9r5rlH.

subject" and how to articulate struggle and emancipation, struggles against oppression and the class struggle.

To get away from a reductionist outlook that boils everything down to the opposition between proletarians and bourgeois, and to avoid falling into a simple list of the myriad contradictions within a society, we tested the formula of "driving contradictions". To break the stranglehold of abstract strategic models, divorced from historical realities, without losing sight of coherent strategic thought, we reflected on the concept of "concrete and evolving strategy". To avoid falling into the trap of prognosis as a basis of political outlook, we relied on the formula "conscious empiricism".

After revisiting the classic debate (late 19th and early 20th centuries) on plurilinear history, we gradually assimilated the concept of "open history" and its multiple implications. Without questioning "concordances" (such as the fact that in a capitalist society the state is bourgeois), we worked on "mediations" and the specific history of each "case in point" (allowing for the understanding of the many functions of states and the originality of each national state), finally looking into the "discordances" that are particularly characteristic of transitional societies where no mode of production can ensure its dominance (and which means that there cannot be a "workers' state in the same sense as a bourgeois one). The work undertaken in the 1980s on these "discordances (in space or time, or among instances) that condition political activities, above and beyond traditional "concordances", continued into the following decade and is till going on today.[16]

The 1980s also saw a revival of criticism of the concept of "progress", of its linear nature, not to mention its inevitability, which had marked most of the previous generations of Marxists.

---

16   See in particular, on this subject, works by Daniel Bensaïd and Michael Löwy.
For Daniel Bensaïd, see in particular the first part of his Marx l'intempestif. Grandeurs et misères d'une aventure critique (XIXè-XXè siècles), Fayard, Paris 1995: 'Du sacré au profane : Marx critique de la raison historique') — and his comments in Walter Benjamin, sentinelle messianique, Plon, Paris 1990. See also on the ESSF website : Fragments pour une politique de l'opprimé : événement et historicité, http://bit.ly/cGKVm5.
For Michael Löwy, see in particular 'La signification méthodologique du mot d'ordre de Rosa Luxembourg 'Socialisme ou Barbarie', in M. Löwy, Dialectique et Révolution, Paris, Anthropos, 1974. 'Histoire ouverte et dialectique du progrès chez Marx', Critique Communiste, Walter Benjamin : avertissement d'incendie. Une lecture des thèses " sur le concept d'histoire ", Paris, Presses Universitaires de France, coll. " Pratiques Théoriques ", 2001.

This also posed (although still too marginally), the correlated need to subject to criticism the productive forces (and not only the relations of production) that characterise capitalism. There we sowed seeds of reflection whose sprouts would mature in the following decade.

This applied in particular to the study of non-capitalist transitional societies — when we had to deal with the lessons of the implosion of the USSR.[17]

Obviously, we were not alone in pursuing our theoretical work and convergences emerged with other critical Marxist currents. This was particularly the case in terms of the ecological question. For many years, we had been involved in a wide range of environmental struggles (against nuclear power or destructive dams, for example) and none of us were unaware that capitalism was destroying the environment. But not until the 1980s did we begin to integrate ecology more systematically into our theoretical corpus and our overall political outlook. (Do note the word "begin"; this process of integration remains incomplete to this day). It was becoming impossible to ignore the scope of ecological issues.

We observed the emergence, for the first time in history, of an "ecological crisis of human origin with a global dynamic" (a type of crisis which in the past had remained local or regional in scope), the consequence of the development of capitalist production and its world market from the 1960s. The development of ideas on this question was no longer the monopoly of "specialists" but entered into the mainstream of the lively debates at IIRE; to such an extent that a decade later, we could play a part in the "plural" affirmation (in convergence with others) of an "ecosocialist" current[18].

---

17   See for example Catherine Samary, 'Mandel's views on the transition to socialism' 1997, published in G. Achcar, The Legacy of Ernest Mandel, Verso, London 2000 (on ESSF: http://bit.ly/bWxLAD See also her comparative study of transformations in the state/relations of property/social relations in Serbia, published in Revue d'Etudes comparatives Est/Ouest, CNRS, Paris 2004, and her articles in Inprecor (August 2006 and December 2006-January 2007 (available on the ESSF website, http://www.europe-solidaire.org).

18   See Pierre Rousset, 'Le Vert et le Rouge face à la crise écologique', 15 March 1998, published in the journal Ecologie et politique, (http://bit.ly/cFGs1J). Daniel Bensaïd, 'Critique de l'écologie politique' in Le sourire du spectre, nouvel esprit du communisme, January 2000 (http://bit.ly/bAxAzc). Michael Löwy, Stathis Kouvelakis, Joel Kovel, 'An Ecosocialist Manifesto' (http://bit.ly/aAGgKo). Pierre Rousset, 'Se laisser questionner par l'enjeu écologique', 30 September 2004, in Ecologie et socialisme, Syllepse (http://bit.ly/doc9cR). Michael Löwy, 'Ernest Mandel et l'écosocialisme',

From gender issues to open history, from ecology to discordances, we can only present a very indigestible and incomplete summary of our brainstorming in the 1980s. All these questions were not foreign to one another; on the contrary, they were part of a framework of critical thought, with an antireductionist Marxist approach as an underlying foundation. They were not purely theoretical, but explored practical implications on the political and organisational level — for example, in terms of the problems of concretely integrating feminist demands into the revolutionary movement.[19]

Unfortunately, in all these fields, a balance sheet of the Institute's first decade largely remains to be written and it is not possible to present a comprehensive view here. But the work done then has had an impact, albeit a diffuse one, on many writings. It is also detailed more explicitly in notes and retrospective studies; we can hope that these will grow in number before an activist generation's memory fades away.[20] The break between the 1960s-1980s and the new century is such that there is no "natural" continuity between yesterday's and today's references. Without a deliberate effort made to pass them on, the critical thinking and self-critical efforts undertaken at the time could easily become diluted and lost. Whatever their limits, that would be a shame.

Fundamental, critical and political education

Developing ideas involves perceiving how things have changed. Since we worked to a great extent on our own experience, this approach was by definition self-critical and was an excellent antidote to temptations of dogmatism. Though we had changed substantially during our first twenty years of activity, other changes were foreseeable in the following decades!

Education at the IIRE was at once fundamental, and in many aspects "classical", but also political and resolutely critical. The length

2005 (http://bit.ly/9DPXE3). Daniel Tanuro, 'Marx, Mandel et les limites naturelles', 19 November 2005, (http://bit.ly/dCp9bD).

19   Penelope Duggan, 'The Feminist Challenge to Traditional Political Organizing', IIRE Working Paper n° 33, 1997, http://bit.ly/dooWoV, and in issue 48 of the IIRE Notebooks for Study and Research.

20   See for example Pierre Rousset, 'Notes pour un séminaire des « formateurs » à l'IIRF : stratégies, contradictions motrices, mondialisation et politique, formes de lutte et partis...,' 10 July 2003 (published on ESSF: http://bit.ly/aBoW62), as well as 'Marxisme(s), révolutions et tiers monde : réflexions sur les expériences d'Asie orientale —Un cheminement générationnel', 15 May2006 (published on ESSF: http://bit.ly/bOCQ13).

of the three-month sessions provided the time to read or reread reference works from Marx's century and from the major revolutionary figures of the following century, while taking up contemporary problems. We were obviously very attached to the lessons of the past and their current validity (such as the terrible lessons on the nature of the state that were provided by the crushing of the Indonesian Communist Party in 1965 and the Chilean Popular Unity in 1973). Without such lessons, we cannot ensure the continuity of struggles, organisations and class independence. But we also learnt to seek out unsolved or new questions, these "questions that question us", that force us to question our own outlook — without losing the red thread of history.[21]

The fact that Marxism was a reference shared by the overwhelming majority of activists of the time facilitated this relationship between education and the development of ideas.

Differences of opinion pertained more to the interpretation of Marxism than to its validity. So we could move fairly quickly from brushing up our "fundamentals" to current debates and a reflection on prospects.

Education and the development of ideas are not mutually exclusive, as if they were two fields foreign to one another. Even elementary education is not unchangeable.[22] It flows from its context.[23] It is a little bit as if every twenty years, the process has to start anew, the "education-development of ideas" cycle must begin again on new bases, based on the outlook of a new generation. Not that the "old guard" no longer has anything worth saying: it is not possible to sweep away

---

21   Overall, the participants and facilitators appreciated this. An initial evaluation was made halfway through and a second one upon concluding. These evaluations were discussed as a group and were positive (daily evaluation sheets on the lectures and the reading material were also filled in by the participants). But some session outcomes could be surprising. For example, a Danish participant thanked us warmly for allowing him to understand how much he liked to study — and concluded that he would cease his political activity to devote himself fully to study! Which was not exactly the outcome we had sought...

22   Certain national organisations had no functioning educational system, and would have liked IIRE to also provide "basic education". This is impossible, as such education depends on the situations and references the participants are familiar with, which vary according to country and generation. There were very few references common to all our session participants — this is one of the inherent difficulties facing us in an international educational initiative.

23   On this subject, see for example: Daniel Bensaïd, 'Thirty years after: A critical introduction to the Marxism of Ernest Mandel'. International Viewpoint Online Magazine: IV392 – September 2007. http://bit.ly/asSeDV

the history of political thought and action. But a critical, and thus self-critical, process is a big help in passing along knowledge and lessons. On condition that the declining generation knows how to expose its own shortcomings and the rising generation knows how to recycle the lessons already learnt.

Figure 12: IIRE Fellow Penelope Duggan, co-editor and co-author of two Notebooks for Study and Research on the struggles of women world-wide

Living our internationalism

Finally, IIRE was and remains and example of concrete internationalism. A place for a synthesis, albeit partial and always incomplete, of an international revolutionary experience.

Beyond political exchanges, living ties of solidarity developed among organisations. Personal links did too, among the participants in a given session, who often stayed in touch once they were back home.

Outside the formal cycle of courses, encounters at the refectory tables and nearby cafés saw many a passionate discussion. Similarly, the regular meetings of the women's commission's were an opportunity, among its other contributions, to take a closer look at the real practices of each movement, the problems they faced, or how women in popular milieus were organised in each country.

IIRE is a project launched and carried forward by the workers' movement. It illustrates the possibilities offered by an international organisation such as the FI, and its potential usefulness. It is also a project open to other currents of the radical, militant left. A dialogue began with these currents, and their participation in the sessions contributed a great deal to us. Up to 20% of the participants came from organisations outside the traditional "borders" of our International - from Castroist, Maoist or semi-Maoist, or "mixed" (product of fusions) currents. IIRE's history, and in particular the history of its first decade, shows us what work in common by radical currents of different ideological origins can be and can provide.

Activists from several organisations coming from the same country might find themselves together for three months during an IIRE session. Sometimes at home, these organisations rubbed shoulders without really talking to one another. In this setting they could often carry on more fruitful debates than they generally had an opportunity to do in their own country.

Thus, in more than one sense, sessions at the Amsterdam Institute represented a living experience of pluralism within the radical left — a pluralism that is also an essential component of internationalism. This type of experience would be worthwhile to take up in other, larger-scale frameworks.

As a cycle ends and a new chapter opens

IIRE's first period was extremely rich in human and political terms. It gave us more than we had hoped for at the outset. Several hundred participants attended the sessions, including nearly 300 to the sessions directly organized by us (we housed others too). But all things, even the best, come to an end.

The initial design of the three-month sessions could not help but be questioned one day or another. This occurred after seven years[24]. It was becoming more and more difficult for non-resident members of the Institute's international team to spend long periods at the In-

---

24 From 1982 to 1988, the IIRE hosted thirteen three-month international sessions. We ourselves remained in Amsterdam for eleven years, up to January 1993. Independently of what we have said in this text about the reasons forcing us to change the design of the sessions, it would probably have been wise to renew the residential staff earlier. It seems that among the Jesuits, responsibilities of this type change every five years. And the Jesuits can be right about some things. Indeed, five years is long enough to give everything we have to give and assimilate the essential elements of what we can receive. After that, there is a risk of falling into routine.

stitute. Work pressures on the resident members increased for this reason, and were unremitting and exhausting. Behind the visible political activities (sessions, publications...) there was also a great deal of hidden administrative tasks, from contacts with the Ministry of Foreign Affairs for visa requests to a thrifty management of everyday budgets. It became impossible to continue at the same rhythm.

The three-month sessions ended earlier than we would have liked. However, a period was ending in any event. With a few exceptions, in the early 1990s, national organisations involved in the Institute's activities had grown weaker. The repercussions of the political "low ebb" of the preceding decade were being felt, making it difficult for them to renew their cadres — and the international teams. It was also becoming harder to free them for such long periods (particularly in Europe). To make matters still more complicated, the important financial contributions which had enabled the international school to operate at full speed started to dry up (once again, this reflected the end of a political period). So we had to make the best of a bad thing, turn a page and prepare for a different type of sessions.

The change in design did not only involve the length of sessions, but also the range of subjects discussed. After the implosion of the USSR and the process of capitalist redevelopment in the Soviet bloc countries, then in China and beyond, of course new angles had to be brought in to the study of transitional societies. The gravity of the environmental crisis became more and more noticeable. Capitalist globalisation was underway. It was time to open sessions centred on these "new questions".

In more general terms, during the international school's first period, reflection on strategy provided the "red thread" that gave coherence to the sessions, over and above the wide range of subjects discussed. The strategic field made it possible to look at questions that had been raised at different steps in the education programme, in a unifying political perspective. All this also contributed to developing real strategic "thought". But, at the end of the 1980s, this strategic thought had reached a plateau, for lack of new revolutionary experiences. Even if none of the lectures had lost its usefulness, a gap appeared between the unifying "thematic backbone" of traditional sessions, the political situation and the new needs of national organisations. We had to look for another "red thread" that could better correspond to the world situation in the 1990s.

Capitalist globalisation and resistance to it would be this new "red thread". In the meantime, the 1989-1992 period was one of transition. One-month sessions, with a tighter programme, were launched. Thematic (economy...), regional (Latin America, Europe, Middle East) or sector-based (women...) seminars and working meetings took on more importance at the Institute. Let us mention, at the time of the implosion of the USSR, a session on transitional societies, with participants coming from Eastern Europe (Poland, East Germany, Hungary). In 1993, a new resident staff took the helm. It wrote the next chapter in the history of the Institute.

Figure 13: IIRE Fellow Janet Habel

Into a new and better century, 1993-2006.
Peter Drucker

When I arrived in Amsterdam to work at the IIRE early in 1993, everyone at and around the institute knew that its work was bound to be affected by the big transformations in the world.

But over three years after the fall of the Berlin Wall and over a year after the collapse of the Soviet Union, we were still coming to terms with the scope of the changes. There was still no solid consensus about the difficulty of the new challenges facing the radical activists and thinkers that the IIRE exists to serve. Some emphasized new opportunities that they thought the disappearance of the Stalinist regimes could bring.

The Sandinistas' electoral defeat in Nicaragua in February 1990 had been one early sign that the whole radical left, including forces with independent traditions and democratic credentials, could be headed for hard times. But other developments were less clear-cut.

Negotiations in South Africa between the apartheid government and ANC were already far advanced, and the end of legal apartheid at hand; the institute's South African co-thinkers would be divided in the run-up to the country's first multiracial elections about the attitude to take towards the ANC-COSATU-SACP alliance. Similarly, the September 1993 Oslo accords between Israel and the PLO would unleash a debate among the institute's co-thinkers in the Middle East. All of them saw the accords as deeply flawed; but some of them thought at first that the peace process could create some openings to work towards Palestinian self-determination.

In the year or two after I began work as programme director at the IIRE, a consensus took shape, slowly and not without frictions, among our Fellows and staff. The conviction took hold that the new opportunities opened up by the fall of Stalinism were dwarfed by the challenges the radical left faced. Only part of the discussion that led to this conclusion took place at the institute itself, of course. Our Fellows were and are part of the leaderships of the workers' movement, its sections and broader political organizations, social movements and left-wing intellectual circles, and the institute was only one place where these debates were taking placed. But as we joined in recognizing the changes in the world, the institute itself changed. In keeping with the critical, open-minded spirit that characterized the institute from the beginning, we helped people on the radical left understand better what was going on, why, how, and how they could resist more effectively.

In the 1980s the IIRE had focused on understanding how post-capitalist societies and states had originated; in the 1990s we helped analyze the consequences of their transition back to capitalism. We produced studies of the new phase of capitalism – the age of neoliberal globalization – that right-wing victories had set in motion years before the cracks in the post-capitalist states became unmistakable. We reorganized our educational sessions to make the challenge of neoliberal globalization their central axis. Not that we presented the challenge in a narrowly economic way; on the contrary, we devoted increasing attention to its ecological, gender, sexual and national/ethnic dimensions, as well as the wars we saw as neo-liberalism's geopolitical expression. In the wake of the 1999 Seattle protests and the rise of the Social Forums, we reoriented our schools and publications to the global justice movement, viewing it as a crucial arena for the renewal of the radical left. And we came to terms – belatedly – with the practical implications of the changes in the world for the IIRE's own operations, a process that culminated in our 2006-07 relaunch.

The backwards transition

Debates over the restoration of capitalism beginning in Eastern Europe were particularly intense. No one associated with the institute regretted the fall of the bureaucratic dictatorships. On the contrary, the IIRE's 1991 seminar on Eastern Europe that Pierre and Sally Rousset mention in their article included Eastern European participants who had resisted and suffered under bureaucratic regimes, for example as part of Solidarnosc in Poland or Charter 77 in Czechoslovakia. As the first democratic governments took office in Eastern Europe, the IIRE even had a friend or two in high places, like veteran dissident Petr Uhl in Czechoslovakia. But in a matter of months the exponents of democratic socialism were unceremoniously shoved aside, often by the apparatchiks of yesterday born again as the capitalists of today. Understanding what was going on took research and time.

And emotions could run high, particularly when it came to countries like Cuba where post-capitalist states continued to survive. When the IIRE opened its doors in 1982, criticism of the Cuban regime coexisted in our circles with a certain degree of enthusiasm for the leadership of Fidel Castro, who had begun as a revolutionary outside the Stalinized Communist Parties and charted a course independent of Moscow. By the 1990s, a long-time student and supporter of the Cuban revolution like IIRE Fellow Janette Habel was striking a more critical note, as in her 1991 book *Cuba: The Revolution in Peril*. The change in tone came by way of some fierce discussions.

I particularly remember an exchange at one IIRE course not long after I joined the staff. Two of the people attending this particular course came from Senegal; they were members of a party that had emerged from largely Maoist roots and acquired a mass base and some institutional weight in Senegalese politics. The day that we discussed Cuba, one of the Senegalese participants said: I have to say that those of us who come from Africa have a hard time discussing criticisms of the Cuban leadership objectively, because of the crucial role the Cubans have played in supporting African struggles. At that point a black South African participant — a fighter against apartheid with a rather light skin whom the apartheid regime had classified as 'coloured' — responded: Well I'm an African too, and I have to say I don't agree with that way of presenting things. The Senegalese rejoined: If you were black, you'd agree with me.

In the discussion that followed neither of them changed the other's mind, either about how to look at Cuba or about who was or wasn't black. Yet the whole exchange took place with mutual respect and even an occasional smile. It has stuck in my mind as a striking example of the institute's success in making it possible to discuss very fundamental differences in a spirit of solidarity and even friendliness. In fact the discussion could scarcely have taken place anyplace else in the world. The Senegalese and the South African didn't even have a common language: the Senegalese spoke French, the South African English, and they could only communicate thanks to our volunteer simultaneous interpreters. Nor would the two of them have been likely to have ever met without the institute, since they were not people who could easily buy plane tickets to other countries — or the kind of people whose travel is often subsidized by governments or major NGOs.

Not only surviving post-capitalist societies generated debate; post-capitalist societies in decomposition were also a source of disagreements. The wars in former Yugoslavia were a notable example, especially the war in Bosnia. Memories are already fading now of how deeply that war divided Europeans, and particularly the left. As it gradually became clear that the US under Bill Clinton and Serbia under Slobodan Milosevic were on a collision course, a number of prominent left-wing intellectuals and currents devoted themselves to refuting, qualifying or evading indictments of ethnic cleansing by Serb nationalists. Others, seeing Milosevic and his allies as the latter-day incarnation of Stalinist crimes, tended to side with the anti-Milosevic forces in ex-Yugoslavia, in some cases even including Croatian president Franjo Tudjman. And of course many on the left adopted the cause of heroic, beleaguered, multiethnic Sarajevo and Bosnia, though they were sometimes a bit taken aback when Clinton claimed to take up the same cause. In those years, well before 9/11, not much attention was paid to jihadis who arrived to fight alongside the Bosnian Muslims after a stint in Afghanistan.

In these many-sided, confused debates, people at and around the IIRE by and large adopted an unusually nuanced position. Credit for this sophisticated analysis was due largely to IIRE Fellow Catherine Samary. An economist who had spent years studying economic self-management in Yugoslavia — her expertise had been put to good use in the IIRE Notebook for Study and Research *Plan, Market, Democracy* — Samary also had a solid grasp of the intricate balancing act that Josip Tito had carried on for decades among the country's different nationalities. Her knowledge made her sceptical of the two most common narratives about the conflict: both the one that described the Western Balkan peoples as being at one another's throats for centuries, only briefly interrupted by a few decades of Communist dictatorship, and the one about the peoples who had lived side by side in harmony until nationalist apparatchiks turned them against one another.

Samary's IIRE Notebook for Study and Research *The Fragmentation of Yugoslavia* had already been completed in French when I arrived. One of my first tasks as IIRE publications director was to see the English edition through to publication. I was impressed by her careful but militant account, which refused either to treat any of the competing ex-Yugoslav nationalisms as innocent or to call down a plague equally on all their houses. Samary's work was an expression of practical solidarity with the Bosnians who were trying to defend the ideal of a multi-ethnic society and at the same time resist the neoliberal transformation of their society. Samary soon developed her vision in greater depth in her book *Yugoslavia Dismembered*. I was glad to help it reach a bigger international audience (and bring in some extra money for the IIRE's always limited budget) by translating it into English for the edition that Monthly Review Press put out in 1995. *Yugoslavia Dismembered* never got the attention given to books on the conflict from bigger publishing houses with simpler plot lines. But I think Samary's book stands up better to rereading than the others.

Ernest Mandel's legacy

The world was not only changing drastically, it was soon the poorer by a major radical thinker: the Marxist economist Ernest Mandel, the IIRE's founding spirit, who died in 1995 at the age of 71. I remembered him well from the week he taught at the three-month course on socialist strategy I had attended in the autumn of 1987. I sometimes wondered how much he remembered about me, hoping in fact that he had forgotten our first meeting. I had been the one to open the institute's front door to him when he arrived for his week's teaching, and never having laid eyes on him before, had suspiciously demanded to know who he was before I let him in.

But I remember his teaching with unqualified pleasure. To my mind, Mandel was not entirely what people took him for. Many people saw him, approvingly or disapprovingly, as a fount of Marxist orthodoxy. His grave, old-fashioned manner suited him to play the part. But his freethinking spirit got in the way. I remember a debate in 1987 about the Spanish Civil War in which students defending different positions implicitly competed for his stamp of approval while he sat listening in solemn silence. When his turn came to speak, he said that he would read to us what 'comrade Trotsky' had written on the question. He then read a very long passage from Trotsky's writings aloud to us, closed the volume, put it aside, and said: 'Now, on the basis of what happened in Spain, you cannot possibly defend what comrade Trotsky says here.' I probably exaggerate in remembering a couple of my fellow students practically falling off their chairs.

One of my last memories of Mandel from my days on the IIRE staff is less pleasant: my memory of his first heart attack, which occurred when he was at the institute for a meeting. I remember his sitting on the steps that led up to the institute library, saying shakily: 'It's nothing, nothing. Perhaps I could have a glass of water. I just need to rest a little, I'll be fine.' But when he got up from the steps it was to be taken away in an ambulance.

It was only fitting that his death provided an occasion to look back critically at his theoretical work over the course of over half a century, which was a significant part of the body of thought on which the IIRE was founded. This critical re-examination took place in particular at a memorial seminar at the IIRE in 1996, a year after his death. The papers presented there were later published as the book *The Legacy of Ernest Mandel* (Verso, 1999), edited and introduced by IIRE Fellow Gilbert Achcar, whose authors (besides Mandel himself) included Fellows Michael Löwy, Michel Husson and Catherine Samary. Written at a moment when optimism on the left was at something of a low ebb, Löwy's essay in particular discussed Mandel's famously incorrigible optimism, distinguishing his occasional over-optimistic judgments from the underlying bedrock of his revolutionary humanist convictions.

Samary's essay took another look at Mandel's conception of the economic transition from capitalism to socialism, showing how after his famous debate with Alec Nove he gradually became willing to allow a greater role for the market in the transition process. On the one hand, she emphasized the constants in his conception of the transition, the things that ensured its continuity and overall coherence: above all the central importance of direct democracy and workers' self-activity throughout the process. On the other hand, she underlined the importance of distinguishing means from ends. Planning, she stressed, is not the essence of socialism, but simply a means to the end of making collective, democratic social choices.

While the market is wholly unsuited to making the major decisions about investments or employment in a transitional society, it can be useful as a mechanism for the allocation of consumer goods — as long as this mechanism is socialized and subordinated to human choices.

The IIRE's commitment to a critical examination of Mandel's intellectual and political work has continued since I left staff, notably in 2007 with the reception at the new IIRE headquarters to celebrate the publication of Dutch historian Jan-Willem Stutje's biography.

IIRE librarian Christopher Beck and I later translated the biography from Dutch to English. The result, *Ernest Mandel: A Rebel's Dream Deferred*, was published by Verso in 2009.

Before my time on staff had ended, yet another long-time IIRE Fellow had died: Livio Maitan. He had been a popular lecturer on topics from Europe to China to the history of the Fourth International. His persistent tendency to go over his allotted time — apparently a surprise to him each time it happened — had been more than compensated by his half century of experience, steadfastness, integrity and shrewd political judgment. It was my successor as programme director, Bertil Videt, who represented the IIRE in 2006 at the founding seminar of the Livio Maitan Studies Centre in Rome.

New questions

A good half of *The Legacy of Ernest Mandel* was devoted to discussing Mandel's work in Marxist economics. His *Marxist Economic Theory* (1962) had helped launch the Marx renaissance of the 1960s by putting Marxist economics on a firmly contemporary, empirical foundation; his *Late Capitalism* (1972) had been a trailblazing account of the nature and end of capitalism's post-war expansion. But clearly by the time he died new changes were visible in capitalism's functioning that Mandel had not yet had time to analyze. In the 1990s a new generation of economists took up this task. Some of them gathered to debate their findings at a series of economists' seminars at the IIRE, which after 1995 took place under the auspices of the Ernest Mandel Study Centre.

As a non-economist I did not participate in these seminars; my then colleague Robert Went was responsible for their practical organization. It's too bad that Robert has not been able to contribute a discussion of them to this volume. For my part I can only report on the aspects of these economists' work that were reflected in the IIRE's own publications and its more general educational courses. We decided in those years to emphasize the newness of the global order we were teaching about by holding several sessions entitled 'new questions'.

Actually the first one was called 'New Questions, New Answers'. But by the time we organized the second one a sense of the magnitude of the issues we were grappling with had made us more modest.

One focus of the IIRE's economic publications from the mid-1990s was debunking mainstream economists' declarations that capitalism had emerged triumphantly from its doldrums and entered a new period of sustained, rapid growth. Looking back, these declarations took a variety of shifting forms, which were sometimes forgotten within a few years. Fellow Tony Smith's IIRE Notebook on *Lean Production*, for example, examined claims that the old Fordist economy had made way for a new 'Toyotist' economy, in which 'just-in-time' production systems would eliminate the sluggishness and inefficiency of the old industrial economy. The economic shifts described were real, of course. Their promise as a basis for long-term growth turned out not to be borne out by the economic performance in the 1990s of their Japanese homeland, however.

The IIRE Notebook on *Women's Lives in the New Global Economy*, edited by Fellow Penelope Duggan and Heather Dashner, similarly debunked the myth that a more flexible capitalism was somehow advancing women's emancipation (except for the small minority of women in rich countries who benefit from the availability once more of cheap servants).

Twelve feminist activists and scholars on five continents described the sweeping changes at workplaces and in families brought about by the growth of world trade, regional economic integration (EU/NAFTA/ MERCOSUR) and austerity policies in response to pressures for 'competitiveness'. They showed how much the new neoliberal order relies on women's cheap labour in dependent countries, flexible labour in rich countries and unpaid labour in homes everywhere. Trupti Shah's fascinating essay on India showed how even that country's plague of 'dowry death', superficially a holdover from its pre-capitalist, Hindu traditions, was in reality the result of capitalist development and the consequent 'Sanskritization' of lower-caste Hindus.

For a large majority of the world's population, in fact, the transformation of global capitalism from the 1980s was most obvious in the human tragedy of the global debt crisis. The IIRE's work on analyzing the changes under way reflected not only an abstract scholarly interest but also a commitment to solidarity with the victims of the process. This commitment was expressed most directly in the 1990s in the institute's partnership with the Brussels-based Committee for Cancellation of the Third World Debt, better known by its French acronym CADTM. This partnership resulted in the IIRE Notebook *World Bank/IMF/WTO: The Free-Market Fiasco*, co-edited by CADTM president and IIRE Fellow Eric Toussaint. It also resulted in practical cooperation on the institute's educational courses. A great proportion of the African participants in IIRE sessions in recent years have come in contact with the institute through the CADTM's work against debt, which has drained their continent of resources and robbed its governments of their economic independence over the past thirty years.

By the time co-director Robert Went's own IIRE Notebook on *Globalization* appeared (in my translation from Dutch) in 2000, glowing accounts of the Toyotist boom had given way to glowing accounts of the dotcom economy. The Notebook exposed the technological determinism behind the standard account of neoliberal globalization, which made it seem as if Thatcherism and Reaganism had been inevitable products of information technology and cheap transport. (Information technology has become increasingly important to the IIRE's work, of course, as Susan Caldwell explains in her contribution to this volume. Cheap international transport would mean more to us if the IIRE wasn't so dependent on fares from the world's poorest countries, which have benefited least.)

Globalization pointed out that political decisions, and political defeats for the left and labour movement, have been crucial to the ways that this technology has been used in society. The account in *Globalization* was actually a prelude to a more thorough discussion in Went's later work *The Enigma of Globalization* (Routledge, 2002), which made clear the qualitative leap involved in today's capitalist globalization by pointing out the unprecedented internationalization of all three of the circuits of capital (trading capital, finance capital and productive capital) described by Marx.

'New' themes

Marxism as understood at the IIRE has never meant a narrow focus on economics, however.

It has always included attention to so-called 'new social questions' — an odd expression, given that the woman's movement for example is at least as old as the modern labour movement. A series of women's schools and seminars at the institute, beginning before my arrival in Amsterdam, has contributed to deepening the radical left's understanding of feminism, as Penelope Duggan recounts in her contribution to this volume. Her Working Paper on 'The Feminist Challenge to Traditional Political Organizing'[25], the distillation of many lectures over many years, is an example of the thoroughgoing, illuminating synthesis of Marxism and feminism that teachers at the institute have brought to bear on many classical political issues. Pierre Rousset, as the institute's first director, was especially concerned with ecological issues; his article discusses this dimension of the IIRE's work.

My own contribution as an IIRE staff person focused on questions of sexuality, which I had been working on for 15 years before I arrived in Amsterdam, and on issues of ethnicity and nationality. I never had any claim to make any original contribution on what Marxists call 'the national question'. I only presented in my teaching what other IIRE associates had researched and written, notably IIRE Fellow Michael Löwy. His anthology : *Fatherland or Mother Earth?* became the first IIRE Notebook for Study and Research to reach a larger audience through part of a series co-published by Pluto Press in London.

This was the second major redesign of the Notebooks during my time on staff. The new-style Notebooks had their disadvantages. For one thing, co-publishing with Pluto sharply raised the Notebooks' price, limiting our ability to distribute them for free or very cheaply in underdeveloped countries and to our own students. The process of negotiating with Pluto at every step of the way also contributed to slowing down the rhythm of Notebook publication.

But most people around the IIRE seemed to feel that the disadvantages were outweighed by the advantages of producing books that really looked like serious books and were read by more people beyond our own circle of contacts.

---

25   Reprinted in "Women's Liberation & Socialist Revolution", a 2010 issue of the Notebooks for Study and Research edited by Penelope Duggan

Fatherland or Mother Earth? was a good Notebook to start with, making an important statement on Marxist debates on nationalism and internationalism. The title made Löwy's internationalism immediately clear: hardly surprising for a writer of Austrian Jewish origin who grew up in Brazil and has been living for many years in France. The book links the tradition of labour internationalism to the new internationalism of the global justice movement and social movements generally, especially the ecological movement (ecology has been another of Löwy's main themes for years). But unlike some Marxist analyses whose internationalism is abstract and expresses a certain disdain for national movements in general, Löwy's argument pays close attention to the specific historical contexts that make some national movements largely reactionary (as often in Eastern Europe since the 1990s) and others largely progressive (from Vietnamese resistance against the Japanese, French and US to the Zapatistas' revolt against NAFTA). He contrasts the aridity of Stalin's four-point definition of a nation — adopted uncritically by a surprising number of anti-Stalinist Marxists — with the insights of Austro-Marxists like Otto Bauer and the flexibility of Trotsky's analysis of African-American struggles in the US, which stressed the importance of the subjective will to national identity.

As the first Notebook in the new Pluto Press series, *Fatherland or Mother Earth?* actually appeared before the last Notebook in the previous format, IIRE Fellow Claude Jacquin's *The Trade-Union Left and the Birth of a New South Africa*. It was no accident that Jacquin's Notebook was published in the old format for a more limited audience. Writing in the wake of the ANC's rise to power, Jacquin was forthrightly critical of the leaders of the former COSATU left. By the time the Notebook was published, several of these unionists had become ministers in the ANC government, without losing their network of contacts on the international left. There were people otherwise sympathetic to the IIRE who thought we were foolish to needlessly alienate leftists in positions of power by publishing this Notebook. I thought it nicely complemented Löwy's discussion of black struggles in the US.

Jacquin had had a good relationship with these 'workerists' when they were still resisting the ANC's attempts to control South Africa's anti-apartheid unions and were trying to develop an anti-apartheid vision linked to democratic, grassroots socialism. At the time they had seen the founders of the Brazilian Workers Party (PT), and even leaders of Polish Solidarnosc, as fellow leaders of another working class on the rise and as co-thinkers in a common, critical socialist project. COSATU leaders' encounter with neo-liberalism gave a foretaste of what the PT leadership would go through a decade later.

Jacquin showed that COSATU leaders' decision in the early 1990s to join the South African Communist Party and ANC went together with an abandonment of their socialist perspective.

Their policies robbed the victory over apartheid of much of its practical significance (e.g. for housing and land) and had disastrous social consequences for tens of millions of black South Africans. Jacquin explained how the end of de jure apartheid in South Africa was compatible with the perpetuation of the society's deep-rooted structural racism.

About the same time, I developed a lecture for the IIRE's 'New Questions' Schools that discussed a non-Eurocentric approach to history. My starting point was the conception of open, plurilinear history that lecturers at the institute in the 1980s like Pierre Rousset, Claude Jacquin and Daniel Bensaïd had stressed as an alternative to the unilinear approach of Stalinized Marxism. Like these earlier lecturers, I underlined the role of human intervention and the specificity of social formations in sending history in one direction or another at decisive moments. I also benefited from the early Women's Schools that Penelope Duggan describes in her article, in which a genuinely international team worked together to further develop a non-Eurocentric feminism.

With these starting points, I tried to take up the challenge to Eurocentrism made by books like Eric Wolf's *Europe and the People Without History* and Samir Amin's *Eurocentrism*.

The lectures examined for example the ongoing debates, which Ernest Mandel had also touched on in his time, about why capitalism had originated in Europe rather than in the initially far wealthier societies of Asia and what the role of slavery and colonialism had been in the process. Even after the rise of capitalist states in the Netherlands and Britain, I argued, capitalism's ultimate triumph on a global scale cannot be understood without connecting its development to the late 17th and 18th-century crises of the Ottoman, Persian, Mughal and Chinese empires. I continue to think that an institute based in Europe, in the midst of societies wrestling with their demographic composition and cultural identities, needs to devote constant attention to such issues.

The second Notebook co-published with Pluto Press — Enzo Traverso's *Understanding the Nazi Genocide* — looked at another crucial period for Europe's history and identity. Here too, unsurprisingly, racism plays a central part. Like Michael Löwy, Traverso sees the 20th century as a watershed in the development of radical thought. The

Marxism of the Second International was infused with a sense of the inevitable triumph of socialism; the radicalism of the 21st century cannot escape a sense of tragedy. Walter Benjamin has taught us to view history from the point of view of its victims, pointing out that 'not even the dead will be safe from the enemy if he is victorious'. Traverso's Notebook, in dialogue with writings on Auschwitz from Hannah Arendt to Daniel Goldhagen, contends that while racial hatred was the first cause of the slaughter of the European Jews in 1941-45, its execution required a 'rationality' typical of modern capitalism.

Sexuality

The study of sexuality (and activism in lesbian, gay, bisexual, transgender (LGBT) movements) has been a constant in my political and intellectual life. Although the Women's Schools always paid attention to women's sexuality, the subject did not occupy a big place in the IIRE's other sessions before I arrived. I was encouraged from the beginning to make room for it, however. Fellow Gilbert Achcar in particular said that I should lecture on the topic at the first session I helped organize at the institute in 1993. Given that the great majority of the students were from Asia and Africa, this meant I had to read and think an enormous amount in the space of a few months. Since I had worked both on issues of sexuality in general before and on the place of underdeveloped societies in the global political economy, I summoned up my courage and plunged in.

This was the beginning of a new direction for me and for the institute that would absorb many of my energies for several years. After lecturing particularly on same-sex sexualities in underdeveloped countries at a number of sessions, I wrote up my approach in an IIRE Working Paper, 'In the Tropics there is No Sin'. These Working Papers were always sent out for comments to several dozen IIRE Fellows and associates; I also sent this one out to people in the field. One of them was David Fernbach, himself the author of the pathbreaking study *The Spiral Path*, an editor at *New Left Review* and one of the founders and directors of Gay Men's Press. Thanks to his support, the Working Paper became an article in *New Left Review* in 1996, which led in turn to the publication in 2000 of the anthology *Different Rainbows*, which I edited and introduced.

Though no bestseller, the book has been praised by important figures in its field. For example, Martin Duberman, Distinguished Professor of History at the City University of New York and the unofficial dean of US lesbian/gay studies, called it 'a unique, long-needed, and immensely valuable book' whose 'significance cannot be overstated', 'brilliantly bound together by the book's editor'. More recently historian John D'Emilio described my introduction as 'one of the best analyses yet written of gay identities and politics on a global scale'.

Figure 14 - Some of the participants in the IIRE's first international LGBT strategy seminar, in 1998

Different Rainbows could never have been written without the uniquely stimulating international environment of the IIRE. The book was only one part of a process of integrating sexuality into the institute's curriculum. Virtually every course had there over the past decade and a half has including one day or more devoted to sexuality; I have been only one of several teachers to focus on the topic (Others have included Terry Conway, Raquel Osborne and Paul Mepschen.) Nor has attention to sexuality been limited to the specific lectures on the subject. IIRE Women's Schools have of course had many lectures linking sexuality to issues like violence and reproductive freedom. Links have been made in other courses as well. Gilbert Achcar's lectures on Islamic fundamentalism have often integrated issues of gender and sexuality, for instance.

High points in the IIRE's work on sexuality have been the international LGBT strategy seminars that took place there in 1998, 2000, 2002 and 2009. They brought together scholars and activists from several dozen countries to study themes too numerous to list, ranging from the family to left history to trade-union work to partnership legislation to HIV/AIDS. Alan Sears of the University of Windsor commented in his report on the 'grounded, practical focus to much of the discussion' at the 2002 seminar, and the participants' sense that it could '"make a difference" in LGBT movements'.

Global justice

From the mid-1990s, the IIRE focused increasingly on neoliberal globalization as the main feature of the times our students and teachers were living through. The economists' seminars and the Notebooks on Lean Production, IMF/World Bank/WTO and Globalization contributed to analyzing the economic side of the process. The 1999 Seattle protests and the rise of the Social Forums made us look more closely at its political implications. As often happens, the change in focus was reflected in new terminology before we were fully able to reflect it in the content of our courses. One year, the New Questions School was rebaptized an 'Anti-Globalization School'. This was of course a poor, first approximation to describing what we were trying to do. The IIRE's staff and students have always been internationalists, and not opposed to internationalization as such. Their problem with globalization is not that it is global but that it is neoliberal, corroding labour's gains and social programmes that were won by decades of struggle at the national level without replacing them by anything remotely equivalent at the regional or international level. After one year the Anti-Globalization School was renamed again to reflect their perspective more accurately, and our series of Global Justice Schools began.

It has taken a certain amount of discussion over several years to make the IIRE's Fellows entirely recast the subjects they were teaching by putting globalization and global justice front and centre. But it has happened, thanks in part to collective reflection at the institute but even more to pressures from the surrounding social and political environment. Through much of the 1990s, intellectual renewal at the IIRE took place in something of a vacuum, in the context of social movements and a radical left that were shrinking and on the defensive. By the end of the decade, though the challenges facing the left remained daunting, debates at the institute were more and more responses to questions being posed in revitalized movements and parties. Increasingly, the activists who attend our Global Justice Schools have been at recent World Social Forums or European Social Forums, and are feeling pressure from the movements to come up with strategic answers.

The 1997 Asian financial crisis set off one wave of social and political events, with for example the collapse of the Suharto dictatorship in Indonesia and recurrent People's Power struggles in the Philippines. Many Filipinos and Filipinas have studied at the IIRE in the course of the past two decades. Many of them found the institute a valuable resource as the long dominant Communist Party of the Philippines went into crisis and its Maoist orthodoxy was questioned from different sides in different ways. Some of our courses in the 1990s included Philippine participants from half a dozen different political currents thrashing out the issues that divided them; in some cases these were people who might not have spoken to one another in the Philippines.

Besides recasting the subject matter of our sessions to fit the era of globalization, we had to change our teaching methods. Participants are no longer willing to accept the course formats that had been acceptable for activists in left-wing organizations in the 1970s and '80s. Now they want shorter lectures, more time to ask questions and more time for discussion. The IIRE's sessions have increasingly featured small discussion groups divided by language, which then come together for plenary discussions with simultaneous translation. Since the most stimulating discussions are often between people from different parts of the world who speak different languages, however, we are often under pressure to shorten the single-language discussion groups and lengthen the plenaries — while we have to watch out not to overwork our indispensable volunteer interpreters! The age of globalization is also the age of internet: Susan Caldwell describes in her contribution the ways she helped the IIRE keep up with its students.

The switch from three-month sessions to sessions of a few weeks has also had many consequences for the practical organization of life at the IIRE. When students were living at the institute for months, it was possible to train them to take on many tasks like cleaning and shopping themselves. In shorter sessions, students often fully master their tasks only about the time they leave. The strain on the institute's small staff — particularly on our first building manager, Michèle Vermeulen, the IIRE's longest-serving staff member — has been far greater. The move to a new building should help moderate this strain, as some of the work can now be shared with the IIRE's partners in the Timorplein complex.

One sad consequence of the move to shorter sessions is that students have had far less time for independent reading. It has been as much as they could do to keep up with the readings assigned for the lectures. This has meant that the IIRE library, which was steadily better organized and computerized in the last years at the Willemsparkweg, was nonetheless less of a resource for the institute's own students. In addition, part of the library was competing for room with the IIRE staff's office space. This too has changed at Timorplein, where the library has its own, completely autonomous space. Cooperation with the nearby International Institute for Social History should also make the IIRE library more accessible to outside researchers — a task that can be tackled now that the tremendous work involved in moving and reorganizing the thousands of volumes has been completed.

Figure 15- Visitors consulting part of the French-language section of the IIRE's library

Porto Alegre

The Asian and particularly Philippine students engaged in an extraordinary process of cross-fertilization at a number of IIRE sessions with students from Latin America, particularly Brazil. The Brazilian Workers Party had been represented in the institute's courses from its first years. The PT founded its own tradition on the Latin American left, neither orthodox Communist nor Maoist nor Trotskyist (though several Trotskyist currents always played a significant role in it) nor social democratic. Its activists' radical and open-minded approach was significant in shaping the IIRE's atmosphere. Particularly left-wing PTers from the southern Brazilian city of Porto Alegre, who were developing their city's participatory budget in the 1990s, came in significant numbers to the institute to explain their innovative project to radicals from other continents and respond to the critical-minded questions they were asked. When the first World Social Forum was held in Porto Alegre in 2000, we had students at the institute from the de facto capital of the global justice movement.

This meant that the Brazilian trade unionists and local officials who came to study in Amsterdam were dealing with some of the thorniest strategic and political issues to face the global justice movement. These students were not only social activists and practitioners of a new experiment in grassroots local democracy; they were also cadre of a political party contending for national office. And they were engaged in intense debates about the PT's programme and direction. In the autumn of 1998, I remember, the Brazilians at the Global Justice School were still confident and enthused at the prospect of an election victory for the PT's presidential candidate Luis Ignacio da Silva (Lula). As supporters of the PT's left wing, they found Lula himself too moderate; but at that moment the left wing had a majority (briefly) in the party's leadership bodies, and they thought they could hold Lula to their party's radical programme. But Lula lost by a hair that year. By late 2002, when he won the presidency on his fourth try, the PT right wing was firmly in control of the party apparatus, PT members were much more polarized, and left-wingers were more uncertain and anxious.

It was during the first months of the Lula government in 2003 that the IIRE/Pluto Press Notebook *The Porto Alegre Alternative: Direct Democracy in Action* was written, edited and published. I had come to know its editor, Iain Bruce, as one of our volunteer Spanish-English interpreters at Global Justice Schools. When Brazilian students spoke in 'Portuñol', it soon became clear that Iain's Portuguese was even better than his Spanish, and that he himself had a wealth of knowledge, experience and contacts in the PT. As Lula's victory approached, the institute's staff and Iain made plans for a Notebook that would capture the best and most radical aspects of the PT's record in office in several Brazilian cities, making this the basis for a possible radical programme for the PT at national level in the framework of a transition to socialism.

Looking back several years later as Lula completes his second term, many on the international left are quick to say that the PT's project was always inherently reformist, and even that the participatory budget was never anything more than a clever radical-sounding device for imposing IMF-style austerity. The IIRE's insistence on seeing history as open and plurilinear suggests that there may have been another way, and that the participatory budget could have had far more radical potential on a national scale if the PT leadership had had the political vision and will to defend it. But the PT's tragedy is illuminated by reading down the table of contents of *The Porto Alegre Alternative* and seeing what has become of its contributors.

Those who held office in Porto Alegre are obviously out of office now, since disenchantment with Lula's administration cost the PT control of Porto Alegre city hall. Some of the contributors are still PT members, though the PT's policies in government today offer little scope for participatory budgets as the Notebook described them. João Machado, who wrote the concluding chapter on the participatory budget and the transition to socialism, is a leader of the Socialism and Freedom Party (PSOL), the main Brazilian party challenging the PT today from the left.

The story of *The Porto Alegre Alternative* has an interesting epilogue, situated at the Caracas gathering of the pluricentric World Social Forum in early 2006. Editor Iain Bruce, who has spent much time in Venezuela in the last few years, organized a workshop in Caracas on the participatory budget, co-sponsored by the IIRE. With the spread of left-wing governments in Latin America, many of the international left have adopted Hugo Chavez — the man who dared to stand up to George W. Bush — as their alternative to Lula, who had cosied up to Bush.

As Chavez' Bolivarian revolution has deepened, however, the question has arisen to what extent the process still depends on the president's own initiative. Can the poor Venezuelans who saved Chavez' government from a CIA-backed coup also take more power into their own hands and more initiative in transforming Venezuelan society? In this sense, the experience of Brazil's participatory budgets may be of some use for the broader Latin American left.

Clash of barbarisms

In the roller coaster of my years at the IIRE, the high of Seattle in 1999 and the first Social Forums were followed by the shock of 9/11 in 2001. Fortunately, at least in Western Europe and Latin America, the global justice movement proved capable of not only surviving the 'war on terror' but of becoming an organizing centre for the antiwar movement. And the rise of the global justice movement in Asia has occurred mainly since 9/11, with the WSF in Mumbai in 2005 as a big leap forward. But events since 9/11 have made clear that the movements and the left face the continuing challenge not only of neoliberal economic globalization, but also of what some have called 'armed globalization': imperial wars in Afghanistan, Iraq and elsewhere.

Figure 16- IIRE Fellow Gilbert Achcar

In this field too the IIRE has done its part to help orient the movements, in large part through the work of Fellow Gilbert Achcar. Of course every course since 9/11 has included discussion of the 'war on terror', usually introduced by Achcar's lectures (though I have occasionally taken his place at Youth Schools). We have reached a wider audience with a number of books, beginning with Achcar's *The Clash of Barbarisms: September 11 and the Making of the New World Disorder*. Published by Monthly Review Press but distributed to the institute's Notebook subscribers, *The Clash of Barbarisms* traces the rise of anti-Western Islamic fundamentalism to US policies aimed at controlling the oil reserves of the Middle East, particularly Saudi Arabia, the 'Muslim Texas'.

Analyzing the disintegration of class-ridden Middle Eastern so-cieties, Achcar shows how US policies fuelled this disintegration in the past and is raising it to new heights of destruction today.

Clash of Barbarisms was only the first of several works that have made Achcar well known to antiwar activists around the world. More recently he collaborated with the writer who is probably the best-known analyst of the US imperium, Noam Chomsky, on a book of dialogues between them called *Perilous Power* (Zed Books). In be-tween, in 2004, Monthly Review Press collected and published Ach-car's essays on the Middle East of the past quarter century in the an-thology *Eastern Cauldron: Islam, Afghanistan, Palestine and Iraq in a Marxist Mirror. Like The Clash of Barbarisms*, parts of *Eastern Cauldron* were translated from the original French by me on IIRE staff time. The volume includes two of Achcar's most important and best known short works: his theses on Islamic fundamentalism, writ-ten in the aftermath of the Iranian revolution, and his 'Letter to a Slightly Depressed Antiwar Activist' just after Bush's 2003 proclama-tion of 'victory' in Iraq.

Analysis of the Middle East by the IIRE's associates has not been limited to Achcar's works.

Israeli activist Michel Warschawski's *Toward an Open Tomb: The Crisis of Israeli Society* (Monthly Review Press, 2004) is another book that I translated on IIRE staff time. At one time we even hoped to organize a seminar at the institute that would bring Achcar and Warschawski together with many Palestinian solidarity activists from a number of countries.

Unfortunately practical and financial obstacles — and some strongly held disagreements among those we hoped to invite, which do often arise even among those on the same side of Middle East is-sues —prevented the seminar from taking place while I was on staff. But I was delighted to attend it at last in 2009.

Renewed vision

Many of the central themes around globalization and global justice were addressed systematically at the IIRE at our July 2003 Fellows' seminar. Given the many other commitments of the institute's lecturers, this was the first chance for many of them to discuss some of the issues in depth with one another. The weekend of intensive discussions in Amsterdam resulted in a renewed curriculum and vision for the Global Justice School later in 2003. The importance of these discussions for the IIRE's work justifies citing the report of the seminar here at length.

Discussions of globalization on the left begin with the understanding that capitalism has always been international and often getting more international. So what's new? Economist Bruno Jetin summed up our Fellows' consensus at the seminar: there are new aspects compared with earlier periods of internationalization (e.g. 1896-1914); but globalization is not a completed process that has made national markets and states irrelevant.... In a whole series of industries (high-speed trains, pharmaceuticals, etc.) the only market on which research and development costs can be recouped is the world market. But everyone agreed that no multinational today is truly 'footloose', truly autonomous of any single national market. Jetin raised the question of whether the process of internationalization and concentration of capital will continue until there are only two or three companies dominating any given sector of the economy (given that the US, European Union and Japan will presumably each insist on having a multinational "of its own" in key markets)....

If today's globalization is unprecedented and even irreversible, then that undermines some of the radical strategies put forward in the global justice movement. [Some say] that the nation-state is still the privileged site for democracy, so that a strategy for economic democracy has to be nationally based and require a high degree of national economic self-sufficiency; and secondly that diversity is a good in itself, so that more uniformity across the world is necessarily a bad thing. Jetin criticized these arguments as being blind to class and gender dynamics, treating national 'communities' as monolithic, and exaggerating the progressive character of the nation state.... Strategies for social transformation must move more quickly than ever before from the national level to the regional or the international and global level....

Who will transform society?

Labour remains a key actor in the scenarios for social transformation discussed at the IIRE; that makes updating our analysis of labour crucial. IIRE co-director Susan Caldwell focused on the sex-segregated nature of the workforce and the gendered structure of the globalization process through the maquiladoras, sex trade, etc. She also raised the issue of the family as the primary location of working class solidarity and the increasing radicalization of workers and women's movements in the advanced capitalist countries, based on the reality that our children's future is a step backward from what the previous generation had achieved.

Fellow Claude Jacquin introduced a discussion of how changes in capitalist production and corporate restructuring have drastically changed the face of the working class. Corporate restructuring has led to a process of industrial deconcentration and segmentation of the proletariat, with workers in different categories and regions having increasingly different situations and even to some extent different interests. This raised questions in some participants' minds — beyond our already existing consensus (formulated by Stephanie Coontz) that class is not the only 'moving contradiction' in patriarchal capitalism — of in what sense the working class is still the central subject of social transformation today.

There is no unifying identity common to all the forces joining in the global justice movement today. That does not detract from the central analytical importance of class. Socialist feminists have always made a key distinction: the autonomy of the women's movement from class and political organizations does not mean its autonomy from class struggle. But that does not automatically resolve the issue of whether a new unifying identity will emerge for today's movements, unifying class, gender, 'civic' and 'human' identities, and if so how and what form it could take....

The lack of a unifying identity in the global justice movement also complicates the question of democratic organization. Former IIRE director Pierre Rousset defended the global justice movement in the seminar against charges that it is undemocratic. Our conception of democracy is too much based on the old 'representative pyramid', he said, or on a juxtaposition of the old representative pyramid to an old model of direct democracy.

Networking meets a need of the constantly expanding and shifting movements today that neither the representative pyramid nor simple direct participation ever could. Efficiency is not the central issue here; inclusion is, so as to sustain the dynamic of the movement. Even 'network' is an inaccurate concept as networks are usually composed of equals while the global justice movement is made of radically different components from individuals to mass organizations.

What then is the role of the party in all this, Rousset asked? One answer was that political organizations embody the choices that movements need to make. As Fellow Penelope Duggan pointed out, this does not necessarily mean that the party is the privileged place where programme is developed. We have certainly been aware since the rise of the women's movement in the 1960s and 1970s that we must take on board the programmatic and analytical developments made within such movements but the party consciously strives to develop a programme that defends the interests of the majority of society. This leaves the question open whether the party must still ultimately be the 'keystone in the seizure of power'....

A different kind of politics

IIRE co-director Peter Drucker defined a further series of political challenges that the radical left is facing, particularly in light of experiences like the *argentinazo* (Argentinean revolt of December 2001) and Lula's presidency in Brazil. How can the left make an idea of politics credible to people that would be fundamentally different from the failed or inadequate politics of reformism, vanguardism and the rejection of politics by anarchistic currents in the global justice movement? The neoliberal state order lacks the capacity to manage resistance movements by buying them off with concessions, as the welfare state used to do. But the capitalist order survived the rebellion and crisis of the past two years in Argentina through a whole set of other mechanisms at the neoliberal state's disposal for defusing resistance: cooptation through subsidies, marketing, polarizing the population along ethnic, communal or traditional political lines, manipulating the rules of the political game, and outright fraud. The radical left needs to insist on the continued necessity of developing medium-term political alternatives and not abandoning the political terrain, Drucker argued, while distinguishing its politics more clearly and explicitly from the kind of failed reformism represented today by Lula in Brazil on the one hand and various, sectarian, self-proclamatory vanguards on the other....

The Global Justice School that followed this Fellows' seminar was reshaped in various ways as a result of its work. For example, lectures on gender, peasantry and ethnicity were brought together in a bloc on 'globalization and social recomposition', with a stronger focus on developments in the global working class. The section on the new world imperial order linked the discussion of US wars and world domination more clearly to the world's economic architecture, international institutions and regional blocs, and was followed by a section on 'globalization and political representation: movements, parties and rethinking democracy'.

The already existing section on 'confronting neoliberal globalization, the globalization of resistance', finally, included more concrete discussions of alternative trade and financial policies.

Fortress Europe

All this work at the institute was done over the years in increasingly difficult conditions.

When the IIRE's founders decided to locate it in Amsterdam, they were relying on the Netherlands' reputation for tolerance for dissent and hospitality to dissenters from other parts of the world. Although the country's reputation has been only somewhat battered in the intervening years, the reality has changed very much for the worse. Pressure from the rightwing VVD in government from 1994 to 2002 and anti-immigrant rhetoric from its leader Frits Bolkestein (later notorious as the European Commissioner who did his best to push through the EU Services Directive in a form as damaging as possible to labour) began the process. In the wake of 9/11, the brief political career in 2002 of right-wing populist Pim Fortuyn and a series of right-wing governments since 2002 have exacerbated it. The result, according to European immigrant rights advocates, is that Netherlands together with Denmark now has the most restrictive laws on immigration and asylum of any EU member state.

The effect on an institute like the IIRE, which depends for its functioning on having students come for courses for periods of a few months or weeks, has been terrible. Most Europeans and North and Latin Americans do not need visas to come to the Netherlands, luckily. But most Asians and especially Africans do. The adoption of the Schengen agreement has meant that any one Schengen country can block entrance for any applicant, with appeal being virtually impossible in practice. Where a visa could often be obtained twenty years ago in a matter of days, many weeks are now often necessary, together with the careful preparation of a file. And that is sometimes not enough for an applicant who is the wrong age, has the wrong job or even lives in the wrong country. The system is geared to admit middle-class professionals. Young activists living among the peasants or poor people they organize, excellent candidates for IIRE courses, simply do not qualify as students in the eyes of immigration bureaucrats. And for years the chances of bringing in participants from a country like Algeria — feminists defending women's rights against both the government and the fundamentalist opposition, sometimes at risk of their lives, for example — were zero. The Dutch authorities demanded that we cough up several thousand euros per applicant as a guarantee of their return home, which the IIRE simply does not have to spare.

The immigration bureaucracy has not been the only one complicating our lives. Several years ago two bad fires in the Netherlands prompted a crackdown by fire inspectors. When the institute opened its doors in 1982, its building complied fully with the existing fire code, and a permit was issued with no problem. In later years each visit of the inspectors could bring unwelcome news that new requirements were being imposed. At one point a new, state-of-the-art fire alarm system was demanded: thousands of euros to install, thousands of euros more each year to maintain it — and simply to be allowed to have it! An urgent appeal to the institute's donors brought in the needed funds. But in 2005 the process reached its ineluctable end: our building simply could not get its permit renewed to house students without ripping out and replacing all our staircases at a completely prohibitive cost. Since we couldn't bring in students from other countries without housing them somewhere, and we didn't have the money to house our students elsewhere, there were several months when we could no longer hold any courses.

By that point, in any event, we knew that we would not be staying much longer at the IIRE's original building on the Willemsparkweg near the Vondelpark. Our move to a new building on Timorplein, in the eastern Amsterdam borough of Zeeburg, was already being planned — in the nick of time.

A new start

The decision to move to a new building was the culmination of many years of budgetary difficulties. The IIRE at its old Willemsparkweg headquarters had in fact never been meant as a paying commercial proposition. Dutch state or corporate funding was never likely for an institution with our outlook. The original building was bought and the institute's operations made possible by generous donations from people who understood our mission and were willing to support it. Unfortunately, by the mid-1990s there were not enough of these people around any more. Essentially, the institute stayed afloat during its last decade on the basis of financial stopgap solutions. Mainly, although the accommodations and meeting facilities we had to offer were far from luxurious — they had been built with our own, rather Spartan ethos in mind — we sometimes managed to find renters among NGOs who took advantage of our excellent location, low prices, service and charm. This became a financial mainstay. But the Willemsparkweg building simply had not been designed for this kind of operation, nor had our staff been trained to run it. It could not be sustained indefinitely.

Figure 17- Gerry Foley, Joanna Misnik and Peter Drucker (right) in 1998

The Timorplein project in Zeeburg, discovered by IIRE board chairman Joost Kircz, provided a way out of our impasse. Supported by the local council, it includes a hostel with hundreds of beds, a restaurant, café, cybercafé, theatres ... designed and run by professionals to professional standards. By selling our Willemsparkweg building and buying a relatively small percentage of the Timorplein space, the IIRE acquired the room it needed for its classrooms, auditorium, library, offices and student accommodations, while having all the other facilities it needed conveniently close at hand. Cooperative agreements signed with other Timorplein partners enable IIRE staff to benefit from our partners' professional expertise while focusing on our own educational core business. All this was new for us, of course; there were a hundred and one details to work out in practice. But the key elements of a workable future for the IIRE are now present, whereas before they were absent.

A few months before the institute moved out of its old building on the Willemsparkweg, I moved on to another job, after 13 years at the IIRE. The Jesuits whom Pierre and Sally Rousset cite in their article would have said that I had overstayed my ideal five-year term.

Looking back, I think that my most significant contributions were made in my second five years: guiding the institute through the aftermath of Seattle and 9/11, organizing the LGBT seminars, launching the book series with Pluto Press. But 13 years was certainly longer than I meant to stay. An institute with such a small staff needs to plan these transitions many years in advance to bring in new blood while ensuring an essential minimum of continuity. And because the IIRE does not lie on any mainstream career path, finding new jobs for departing staff and finding new staff to replace them is always a prolonged and challenging process.

Going off staff has not meant the end of my responsibilities. The IIRE's work has never been done by its paid staff alone. It was and is part of a broader radical left movement; its teaching, writing, editing, translating and much more are done by the unpaid activists who make up that movement. The demand for changes at the IIRE has come, ultimately, from them, in response to the major changes in the world they have faced over the past two decades. Clearly more changes are ahead for the left and the institute — now, let's hope, for the better.

One change now in progress was foreshadowed in my last months at the institute, as I began work on one last Notebook. I wanted a book that would disseminate the debates between prominent theorists of one wing of the global justice movement — people like

Toni Negri and John Holloway — and IIRE Fellows like Daniel Ben-saïd and Michael Löwy. My successor as IIRE publications director, Murray Smith, saw the book into print under the title *Take the Power to Change the World*.[26] Its appearance signaled the return of the big questions of political strategy that (as Pierre and Sally Rousset say in their article) were at the centre of the IIRE's discussions in the 1980s, but receded into the background in the 1990s. I am sure the IIRE can address them as creatively and critically in this new period as it did in the past.

---

26   NSR 37/38 Take the Power to Change the World, Phil Hearse ed.

My four years at IIRE.
Susan Caldwell

I came to the IIRE in 2000 with a limited 4-year tenure, as I was on leave from my teaching position in Montréal, Québec, Canada. I came to the IIRE with a professional background in teaching and curriculum development, including web-based courses, and a political background of being on the leadership of the various Québec and Pan-Canadian organisations and on the Women's Commission of the FI. I had never attended one of the 3 month schools at the IIRE but had been one of the team that led the 1997 Women's School.

Thus I came with great enthusiasm and one clear project – to get the IIRE on the web. In my view, the necessity of getting the IIRE on the web was in part due to the new development of the World Social Forum processes – and other international progressive responses – that used the web to organise, coordinate and distribute a political understanding that 'there is an alternative'. With travel costs in Canada being prohibitive due to its geographic size, the Pan-Canadian organisations had been successfully using e-mail and websites for a number of years to carry out coordination and discussion tasks, within the context of a bi-national and bilingual Canadian state. The IIRE faced and faces similar challenges – the high cost of bringing activists together from around the world for an extended period – 1 to 4 weeks – and of functioning in three languages – Castilian, English and French. All schools were conducted in two languages – English and French or English and Castilian – which added to the cost and complexity but also added to the interest in the discussion and analysis. I thought having a website would help prepare people for the schools and offer the chance for continuing the discussions after the schools. So working with Ailko van der Veen, we created a webpage for the schools. This was successful at providing an archive of the readings and resource material for the various schools but did not really serve to provide a means of discussion afterwards. Most of the presentations were in lectures, often in a 'cours magistral' style[27]. While this can work well in a face-to-face context, without the support of a written outline, hopefully including a visual component, online users get lost.

Creating a web page meant that all presenters began to understand and develop supporting documentation, including outlines, readings that could be downloaded and links to other relevant website.

---

27 A one-way lecture, with minimal questions and discussion

Recordings had always been made of the lectures – and their translations – with participants making copies of the tapes to take back to their countries.

I think that the challenge of using IT – information technology – continues, with new possibilities developing all the time. To take one example, when I left in 2004, it was still rare for an academic institution to offer audio recordings of classroom lectures free to their students, but now a rapidly increasing number of universities offer free podcasts linked to free podcast subscription software. While only one-direction – from source institution to user – this form of information technology can provide another means for the distribution of the presentations done at the IIRE.

In contrast to the first decade of the IIRE, during my four-year term, presenters usually came only for a day or two, thus limiting the possibility for collaborative discussion with the participants and the staff. One of the most satisfying moments was the meeting of the Fellows in 2003 which allowed for at least a weekend of the sort of exchange that was part of the school in the first decade (see Pierre's report). Peter has given the summary of this meeting in his report. One of the challenges facing the IIRE and its Fellows is finding a way to use information technology to facilitate some of this necessary exchange of ideas. Pierre's ESSF website plays an important role in accumulating critical essays and reports, but that is just the beginning.

Since the 1990s, the political situation for traditional international organisations has radically changed, with the development of other forms of international and transnational organising which escaped the limits of the UN based international meetings, such as the series of women's meetings begun in 1975 in Mexico. For example, the Fédération des femmes de Québec launched the World March of Women against Poverty and Violence 2000 following the 1995 UN women's conference in Beijing. In October 2000, women organised and marched in 87 countries around the world. They also conducted regional marches in Europe and North America and global marches in Washington, DC and in New York to pressure the UN. In January 2001, the first World Social Forum was held in Porto Alegre, Brazil to counter the arguments and propaganda from the World Economic Forum which regrouped the leaders of the capitalist world at Davos, Switzerland. This process of international and regional social forum encounters created a political context in which the education that the IIRE offered could gain added significance. The IIRE's three-week-long Global Justice Schools provided an opportunity for activists within the social forum process to discuss theory, strategy and experiences with like-minded people from other countries.

The Global Justice School in 2003 was particularly significant for its African and Philippine participation, an exchange that would have been hard to achieve by any other means. The Women's meetings of 2001, 2002 and 2006 provided the same opportunity for women to discuss the development and strategy of both their regional and the global women's movements. The Youth Schools offered younger activists from Europe the opportunity to develop a greater theoretical understanding of their activist politics.

All of these face-to-face experiences create the human bonds that are the central reality of an international. In the context of a continuing process of international and global activism, the role of the schools conducted at the IIRE is all the more important.

Figure 18 Former IIRE co-director Susan Caldwell

My four years at the IIRE were wonderful for me on the personal and political level. As a single parent, raising a son, I couldn't take off the 3 months to attend one of the original sessions. These four years gave me the opportunity to meet several hundred activists from around the world, to teach and learn from them. I had attended various international Fourth International meetings since 1987, including a 5 month stay in France, attending LCR meetings. Now I was able to attend the meetings of the groups in Germany, Sweden and Switzerland, and with each group I learned more about the social reality behind their political analysis. Having come from

Québec, I was invited by the coordinator of the World March of Women in the Netherlands, Charlot Pierik, to take part in the international meetings of the WMW in Rome and to represent them at the World Social Forum in Mumbai in 2004.

Since the 1997 Women's School, I have been developing lectures on women and globalisation. Clearly my work with the World March of Women reinforced this thinking.

However, a radical shift in my perspective came about in 2004 while taking part in the Tri-People Grass-root Women's Peace Exchange in Mindanao, the Philippines, organised by Eva Ferraren of Sumpay Mindanao International. I was to give my lecture on 'women and globalisation' at a closing seminar after two weeks of 'exposure' to the situation of the Lumad, Moro and Christian settler women and organisations. What became clear to me was that my lecture did *not* really reflect either their analyses or their experience, as the role of the state (or lack of it other than as a military presence) and the issue of development required a serious supplemental analysis of a strategic perspective for this situation. I reworked my PowerPoint presentation, which the women found very useful. They asked me to repeat it to another audience and translated it into several of the local languages. While clearly not all programme directors can have such an opportunity, this experience fits perfectly into the logic and ambitions of the IIRE in creating the type of political exchange that leads to new thinking for the revolutionary challenges we face.

Seeing the world through the eyes of the women and youth.
Penelope Duggan in collaboration with Heather Dashner

From the outset, the sessions organised in the IIRE made a point of including at least one lecture centred on understanding women's oppression and the different forms of women's struggle for liberation, and also of integrating this problematic into the sessions in general. [28]

This latter aspect was undoubtedly, given the generation and political formation - and gender - of most of the lecturers, less successful.

It was also, however, a point of principle to encourage women participants, including refusing multiple participants from the same organisation unless the group proposed was mixed, and to encourage women present to meet together to share experiences and build solidarity among them. This was to make it easier to confront the usual dynamics of exclusion and undermining of women in political groups that exist even in groups that have explicitly recognised the ongoing reality of women's oppression and the need for a constant struggle against it. It was particularly necessary given that the experience of many women in the Fourth International is that they have carved out respect and self confidence based on proposing and carrying out tasks, while the basis for relations in the schools is political and theoretical debate, usually a particularly thorny area for women This was undoubtedly the case of the core (FI) groups participating in the sessions, even if it was in itself an educational process for most activists, but particularly for other groups which had not yet taken on board these programmatic points.

However the understanding and ideas that were brought into play during the first ten years of the Institute drew their inspiration from the discussions that had been provoked by the rise of the second wave of the women's movement in the 1970s and were codified in the resolution adopted by the World Congress of the Fourth International in 1979.

By the time that the three-month sessions came to an end there was a general feeling that there was a need to relaunch the programmatic and theoretical discussion that had run out of steam in the 1980s.

---

28 Penelope Duggan, associate Director with special responsibility for women's and youth programmes in collaboration with Heather Dashner, joint coordinator of IIRE Women's sessions

Thus one of the first projects in the new period of the Institute was to organise a women's seminar. The initial concept was very ambitious and was explained in the following way in the balance sheet written at the time: "The seminar as conceived by the IEC Women's Commission was aimed at advancing the thinking of the International in relation to a number of the discussions underway in the feminist movement. This objective stemmed from a recognition by the women's commission that our current plays little role as a current in these discussions and that they are largely unintegrated into the thinking of the International as a whole.

"Thus the purpose of the seminar was to give our activists who have been involved in leading the women's work an opportunity to share their experience and the development of their thinking in order to collectivise what has been national or even individual development up to now. Like any other leadership educational activity, it was also intended to give activists who normally carry a heavy load of responsibility a period in which to think more freely without being under daily pressure to develop a line or give answers to tactical questions or quite simply to carry out the usual organizational tasks."

The session took place in September 1991, using English and Castilian, with 25 participants; They came from Asia: (5/25) 20%; Africa: (1/25) 4%, Europe: (9/25) 36%; Latin America: (7/25) 28%; US/Canada: (3/25) 12%, 5 of whom who were only present for 1 to 3 weeks of the 4 week session.

However the stated objective turned out to be too ambitious: "The school was successful for having served a different purpose than the one originally posed.

To hold a seminar for a leadership layer corresponding to members of the IEC women's commission would have required a smaller seminar with a more selective approach to invitations. The development of different sections of the International in their size, implantation, history and general level of political formation is too uneven to make it possible to hold such a seminar expecting that every section can participate."

Thus, concluded the balance sheet, the original goal of moving forward collectively in our discussions at leadership level was not reached, but the school had played an important role in bringing together a newer and younger layer of women activists willing to invest themselves in women's work, and in particular in giving them an experience and knowledge of the International and enabling them to form links with other women from other countries on the basis of personal contact.

The school was indeed successful enough to be repeated three times during the 1990s (1993, 1997 and 1998, once using English and French as the vehicle languages).

It also contributed to renewing the content of the "general schools" which in the following fifteen years were variously named "New Questions" or "Global Justice" notably on three points: further integration of the problematic of women's oppression into discussions of Marxist theory, expanded discussion of party and movement using the ideas developed in discussing the autonomy of women's movements, and the dynamics at play inside political organisations in relation to women's participation, which was for a whole period a topic for regular lectures in these schools. The first school to benefit from this renewal was that for "young cadres under 30" in spring 1992.

The content of the 1991 school was outlined as follows: [It] started from a new look at the discussion of the usefulness of Marxism as a tool in understanding and analysing women's oppression — discussions which have continued since the last time our movement touched on them in the 1970s in the context of preparing the 1979 resolution. Then the topics scheduled raised specifically some new discussions which we have never discussed at the International level (philosophy of difference, sexuality, sexist/sexual violence). The last part of the seminar was then to deal with problems of building the movement particularly drawn from the newer experiences since 1979 (e.g. Latin America and South Africa). The last point was a rediscussion of the problems for revolutionary parties in recruiting and integrating women and the problems that women themselves face (how to build "women-friendly" parties).

This basic structure was maintained during the three following schools, although some specific points were changed, added or dropped, for example the introduction of a lecture on women and Islam, or the removal of a lecture on the history of women's struggle for the vote or the panel discussion on the theory of difference that took place in 1991 built was no longer so pertinent in later years.

Figure 19 - Heather Dashner

The discussions provoked at the sessions were many and various but one was a constant theme: the question of "Eurocentrism".

Like many other political and social movements, the best-known experiences, because the best-documented, tend to come from those countries where the technological capacity to document and relay these experiences (whether of movements in action or theoretical contributions) is most developed. This is just as true of the women's movement, and possibly more so as all inequalities tend to become more marked once they are refracted by gender inequality. But, in addition, the second wave of mass women's movements took place first in Europe and the U.S. in the 1970s, which was central to changes in thinking in the FI, and to providing experiences and dynamics which in many cases were very easy to mechanically transfer to other countries, but which also naturally produced enormous amounts of thinking and writing. Therefore much of the material available to us did indeed come from Europe and North America. As the session was located in Amsterdam it was obviously far more possible for us to invite women lecturers from other European countries than elsewhere.

Nevertheless, we made a huge effort, in relation to our very limited capacities, to use resources, both in terms of texts and lecturers, whose experiences and frames of reference were other than European (or North American, which in this debate tends to be assimilated to "Eurocentric" thinking). This was an important political task and we can only have partly succeeded.

However it was also important to point out that explaining and using European or North American experiences as a starting point for the discussions was not necessarily Eurocentric, insofar as the purpose of the "education" at the Institute is not a teacher/taught relationship in which the "truth" is passed on but the opportunity for a critical exchange between equals.

From this point of view, whether the starting point and frame of reference of the lecturer was from Mexico, India or Britain the connection and comparison could be made with the experience of those from South Africa, Canada or the Philippines, so that the understanding of all was enriched and deepened.

What is to be guarded against is the tendency to assume that one's own experience is the "model" and indicates the path that others will take, and indeed one of the original purposes of the seminar was to provide a forum for the development of our thinking in a more international was, although an important step on this road had already been the 1991 resolution on women's and feminist movements in Latin America.

Not all the discussions that animated the women's sessions - which were in fact women-only except for the presence in at least two of the sessions of one male translator and the male staff of the Institute - concerned the political content. Three points in particular were noted in the evaluation of the 1991 session:

"First of all, there were many protests that the personal data sheets that the Institute asks participants to complete did not ask whether or not they had children. It is obvious that this is a question that should be asked.

Second, there were a number of activists who expressed a feeling of being very burdened by the domestic chores. It is obvious that to continue to be tied to the rhythm of cooking, cleaning and washing is more burdensome for women than for men because they are in daily life already mainly responsible for this.

Third, the general rule on visitors was quite strongly challenged. This is the rule that says the only visitors who may stay in the Institute are "companions". This was put into questions for two reasons. The general one is that this is giving a privilege to activists who a) have companions and b) have ones who can come to Amsterdam. The second, more specific to this session, was that the introduction of men into the collective living of a group of women was not very appropriate.

It was felt that the arguments of the need for control over who comes to the Institute and limiting the number of visitors would be met in a more egalitarian fashion by saying that each participant had the right to have one visitor during the session for a limited number of days. Any visitors should be announced in advance and could be refused for reasons of numbers if necessary."

The first and third of these points brought about immediate and uncontentious change to the rules and practice of the IIRE. It is simply surprising that they were only raised after more than ten years of functioning.

However the second point is more interesting to consider. In the first place obviously the extremely limited budget of the IIRE simply ruled out having staff who would prepare meals or do the cleaning. However secondly, for us it was an important political point that should be understood by all - especially the men - who attended sessions that such tasks exist and have to be done, and everybody has to participate. Some interesting experiments in teaching how to clean bathrooms or cook meals occurred!

In at least one other women's session however, cooking became not a chore but a competitive sport and participants had to be reminded that showing off the best dishes from "home" was in this case less important than participating in the discussions.

The women's schools had been launched as a joint venture between the IIRE and the Women's Commission, which took on the major responsibility for developing the programme of the schools, finding the lecturers and reading material and provided at least two full-time "session staff" for each session.

After 1998 this body was no longer in a position to provide the resources to organise this sort of session and such a session has not been held since then.

However in 2006 a week-long seminar was held. Although the participation was as heterogeneous as ever the content was conceived quite differently:

The form of the seminar was something that we rarely try to do: to reflect on our past experience and practice in a systematic way.

Our goal was to understand the development of our women's work and the debates and resolutions it had provoked in a particular historical period - in fact since the rise of the second wave of the feminist movement (1970s)

An introductory report was prepared by two activists who have participated over the last thirty years in the Women's Commission of the International in order to situate and trace the development in our thinking at an international level (notably through World Congress texts).

As this Commission has not functioned as a really representative body since the late 1990s this drew largely on the experience of collective work of the late 1980s and 1990s.

We also asked three countries to prepare reports on their experience: France, Brazil and the Philippines.

The reason for this choice was that these are three countries where our national organisations still have organised women's work - this is not the case for all sections - and have a historical experience of it as an organisation. In addition, coming from three different continents and emerging at different periods of the FI's history they also brought a number of other factors into the discussion: the difference in the development of the women's movement and the way questions of women's liberation are posed, different political and cultural traditions.

The seminar concluded with a day's discussion of the experience of all the participants as women militants in their own organisations and then finally with an attempt to draw some conclusions on the themes that should be dealt with in future IIRE sessions devoted to the questions of women's oppression and women's liberation.

Youth schools

The proposal to hold special sessions for youth leaders from Europe emerged after some ten years of the annual youth camp. This camp was first held in 1983 in Germany and has been maintained as a regular initiative of the youth organisations and sectors in Europe bring together several hundred young people for a week of "politics and partying" every July. It is planned and organised by the international meetings of representatives from the delegations, while the logistical back up is given by the Fourth International organisation in the country where it is held (it moves from year to year). This initiative draws in particular new young people, on average the "first-timers" comprise 60 per cent of the camp. From this point of view the more experienced youth in each delegation have a role of leadership and accompaniment of the newer and less experienced youth, leaving them less opportunity to benefit directly from the political activities, which are indeed mainly addressed to the newer ones.

Figure 20- Some participants at the IIRE's 2006 women's school

This, combined with the ever present need to ensure a new leadership layer internationally, encouraged us to propose a special session whose goal is to encourage the development of such a layer and offers the young activists a chance for intensive international education. It is held every year that it is is possible to gather the minimum number of participants (12-15) that make it feasible.

In the first years the programme tended to be a reduced reproduction of the programme of the general schools. However in 2004 a new proposal was made that started from several considerations:

• the time available for the school is considerably shorter - the best of bad options is to have it at the end of August, knowing that the youth audience has already taken a good week at the end of July to attend the youth camp;

• the youth activists, unlike the vast majority of activists attending sessions of the school have already spent probably several weeks at different camps discussing, in the recent period, globalisation and exchanging experiences with young people from other activists;

• they did not experience, and often know little about, the founding experiences and discussions that formed what still tends to be the dominant leadership layer in the Fourth International - that is the experiences and discussions of the "1968-1974" layer and in particular the discussions on strategy of that period.

So a new programme was formulated that attempted to combine discussing key elements of revolutionary strategy in both theory and practice with real historical experiences, such as the fight against apartheid in South Africa with the concept of permanent revolution, or different strategies for taking power in Latin America, whether Cuba, Argentina, Chile, Nicaragua or Brazil, Venezuela and Bolivia today. It does not of course ignore the need to understand Marxist method, nor the fight against women's oppression, nor the need to build an International.

The enthusiasm and energy of the young activists can leave us wondering, how did we ever do that?- although the 'out to 4 o'clock in the coffee shops of Amsterdam' mode has been known to drive certain co-directors to resort to brutal methods of waking participants at five to nine. On the other hand, certain groups have worried us by their too studious attitude...

However one thing is a constant, one doesn't eat well in a youth school!

2009: A year in the life of the IIRE.
Bertil Videt and Marijke Colle

Globally, 2009 has been marked by the economic crisis, which has turned out to be a systemic crisis for the capitalist world system as such. As this crisis is converging with the climate crisis, the world stage is set for a radical change in global social relations. This constitutes a major challenge for progressive forces around the world, and has required the International Institute for Research and Education to rethink its programmes and curricula. The global crises, and our attempt to analyse them from different perspectives, remained a cardinal point of all IIRE activities throughout 2009.[29]

With no less than four seminars and two longer educational sessions 2009 turned out to be a very productive year for the International Institute for Research and Education.

Seminars and Schools

IIRE Palestine Seminar

From 14-17 February, IIRE held a timely Seminar on Palestine, gathering 29 participants from Lebanon, Israel, Morocco, The Philippines, Canada, France, Italy, Britain, Switzerland, and The Netherlands. The Seminar, conducted with simultaneous translation in English, French and Arabic, was a unique congregation of radical activists working in solidarity with the people of Palestine. Topics such as the imperialist strategy of the USA and EU in the Middle East, the impact of the Zionist project in the region and current Israeli policies laid out the background for an in-depth discussion and assessment of the Palestinian national movement. Furthermore, the debates carried forward to the more long-term prospects for Palestine.

Despite differing in their approaches, the participants agreed on condemning the recent attacks against Gaza and unconditionally supporting the Palestinian people and their struggles: the right to self-determination without any external interference; the right of return for refugees or compensation for those who demand it; and equal rights for the Palestinians, whatever their condition since 1948. To add, the seminar participants reaffirmed their solidarity with the

---

29   This is the 2009 annual report of the IIRE. It gives a good flavour of a year's activities at the Institute.

struggle to dismantle the Zionist state which represents a racist and colonialist project at the service of imperialism, and in favour of a political solution in which all the peoples of Palestine (Arab and Jew) can live together in full equality. Finally, a brief discussion concerning the Palestinian majority in Jordan and the need to dismantle that absolute monarchy was elaborated throughout the four days.

The seminar ended with a commitment to produce a Notebook based on the talks at the seminar and to gather a broader seminar next year. One of the most practical outcomes at the end of this IIRE session was the call to support the Boycott-Divestment-Sanction (BDS) campaign, initiated in 2003 by more than 170 NGOs, associations and Palestinian parties.

For more background on radical views on the conflict, we recommend the reading prepared for the IIRE Palestine Seminar, which can be downloaded from in English and French.

Women's Seminar

"We must do this again - very soon, said one of the twenty-two radical socialist-feminists from eleven countries in Europe, Latin America and Asia, who participated in the IIRE International Women's Seminar, 11-15 July. "It was so positive to have the time to explore these issues together and look at them in an international context."

The main themes discussed during the four days were: the impact of the global economic and ecological crises on women, women and migration, religion and women's oppression, the role of feminists in the anti-capitalist movement and the Encounter of Latin American and Caribbean Women (El Encuentro) held earlier this year in Mexico. Additionally, participants provided reports on the state of women's struggles in their respective countries.

Participants noted that women's experience of the economic crisis was so far very different in different countries in some places it has been mainly male-dominated areas of employment that have been hit with the service sector still to be hit whereas in others, women's rate of unemployment is already rising more rapidly than that of men. Attacks on the public sector which are a common feature of the crisis everywhere, affect women both as workers and as service users and seem set to continue apace. Women are at the sharp edge of the climate chaos as those responsible in many societies for collecting and providing food and water, essentials of life that are becoming more difficult to access in more and more places.

A two-woman delegation from the Philippines presented a talk on the causes and effects of migration in the Global South from a feminist perspective. Here, the vicious cycle of migration, the impact it has upon women (daughters and grandmothers) who stay in the home countries, the economic importance of domestic workers, violence and human rights were discussed in-depth.

In the session on religion, the way that the Turkish state uses Islam and the Vatican uses Catholicism were the starting points for an interesting debate on the rise of right-wing populism, cultural identity and resistance. One of the conclusions that were drawn from the presentations was that religious conceptions of what women should be are continuously being used by the ruling classes to defend their interests - and the so-called liberal democracies of Europe are no exception.

Finally, some reflections on the state of feminism in Latin American were provided by those who participated in the Encuentro. Important issues that sprang from this last experience were the need and possibility to organise as socialist feminists, generation gaps among feminist activists and women rights under the new progressive governments of Central and South America.

The seminar had three purposes. First, to continue the work of documenting the above-mentioned issues and struggles, a task that was set at the last Women's Seminar in 2006, in order to draft an updated Marxist analysis of how women's oppression functions in late capitalism. Secondly, participants aimed at preparing for a solid feminist intervention at the next Fourth International World Congress, in February 2010. Finally, the invaluable experience of sharing perspectives with women from different countries provided a base for strengthening the ties of solidarity. All three objectives were met and a working group for the drafting of theses was set up. A ten-day Women's Seminar is to be organised within the next two years

LGBT Strategy Seminar

All the participants in the fourth LGBT seminar held at the IIRE in July 2009 were extremely positive about what they had gained from sharing the three days of discussion and debate on key issues facing LGBT people working in an anti-capitalist framework.

The 26 participants were from Lebanon, Palestine, the Philippines, India, Brazil, Venezuela and Mexico, Portugal, Denmark, Turkey, Germany, France, The Netherlands and Britain. Shortage of funding as well as visa difficulties prevented still wider non-European participation but nevertheless there was the basis for a real internationalist reflection which many of the participants said was one of the unique things about the event they really valued.

The seminar was broader than previous ones as a result of inviting individuals who are conscious anti-capitalists but not necessarily members of explicitly anti-capitalist organisations. Participants agreed that this should be repeated in organising the next event.

The presence of at least four transgender, transsexual, intersexed people more than at previous events was a positive feature. This led to discussions which were an important element in the seminar's success. The atmosphere was warm and the discussions comradely throughout the weekend.

There were sessions on LGBT self-organisation in the Middle East and the intersection between LGBT organisation and the project of 21st- century socialism in Latin America. Beyond these, perspectives were developed in other sessions, for example on queer theory and politics, and on homophobia and Islamophobia in Europe. They were developed in a less Eurocentric context than would previously have been the case.

There was a consensus on several important conclusions:

A non-Eurocentric approach to sexual oppression and emancipation is important to opposing both the Islamophobic "clash of civilisations" and the fundamentalist-friendly reaction to it by some sections of the left.

In the Latin American processes of radicalisation, notably in Venezuela, insistence on self-organisation by LGBT and other specifically oppressed people is important to the fight for a 21st-century socialism from below, that rejects authoritarian tendencies and the temptation to repeat 20th-century errors.

Where revolutionaries are working in broad radical left parties, it is important to insist on self-organisation within these parties by LGBT and other specifically oppressed people, and that this self-organisation is being reflected in the parties' programmes and practice, as a means of resisting pressures towards electoralism and institutionalisation.

Participants also appreciated the discussion on queer theory and politics, since many radical LGBT activists in some parts of the world work in or with currents who draw on queer theory and queer activism. A presentation explained how queer theorists have deepened the feminist understanding of the social construction of gender - by showing that sex is also to a large extent socially constructed. Such an understanding is particularly important to trans and intersexed people. It also deepened the understanding of how profound heter-onormativity is for the way patriarchal capitalism functions.

Criticisms were also made: for example, that some queer theorists denounce "identity" to such an extent that they risk undermining the political basis for the self-organisation of oppressed groups and that some queer theorists and activists neglect the role of the material power structures of patriarchal capitalism. Nevertheless many participants found that queer theory and activism have a lot to contribute to a Marxist-feminist approach. There was general agreement that the discussion on queer theory and politics should continue.

The only negative comments about the event were that we had insufficient time to discuss individual topics as well as to share personal and political experiences.

Participants decided in principle to hold another international LGBTI seminar in the summer of 2011, hopefully lasting slightly longer.

IIRE Economy Seminar

On 2-4 October, the IIRE held its first international Economy Seminar on the Global Crisis. Thirty-six participants, economists and non-specialists, from Europe, Africa, Asia and Latin America attended the three-day event which was open to activists from different tendencies of the radical left.

The objectives of the seminar were to analyse the nature, characteristics and consequences of the current global economic crisis, from perspectives relevant to social activists, and to fortify the global network of Marxist economists.

Three main questions guided the various sessions of the weekend. First, what is the nature or cause of the crisis? Second, what are the social, economic and political consequences? Finally, what are the links between the current economic crisis and the global ecological and food crises? A solid look at Keynesianism, Ernest Mandel's contribution on long waves and economic cycles and a (self) critical take on discourse and propaganda peppered the debates.

Francis Chesnais (France) opened the seminar with an introduction on the role the so-called financialisation of the economy had in the global crisis. He stated that the crisis cannot be labelled either financial or financialised. Rather, the current crisis has its roots deep in the process of capital accumulation, which, revealing its contradictions, should lead us to look at the dynamics of productivity, the rate of profit and its distribution. The discussion that followed generated a debate between over-accumulation versus under-consumption as explanations for understanding the crisis.

Ozlem Onaran (Turkey), Claudio Katz (Argentina) and Bruno Jetin (France) presented reports on the conditions of the European, Latin American and Asian economies. The debates paved the way for a deeper understanding on how the crisis is perceived and dealt with in the different regions. Participants concluded that an essential characteristic of the crisis is the lack of de-linking tendencies among countries and continents; on the contrary, the efforts to save capitalism have been concerted and almost unanimous.

Michel Husson (France) and Klaus Engert (Germany) analysed the crisis in the framework of the theory of long waves. According to this theory, elaborated by IIRE founder Ernest Mandel, it is possible to use important endogenous factors, i.e. related to the logic of capital and its internal contradictions, to explain the general fall in accumulation that began during the 1970s and has not yet stopped. This discussion left open the possibility of a new ascending wave of economic growth and capitalist accumulation dependent on such exogenous factors as a radical change of the relationship of forces between the classes. One of the conclusions, therefore, was that another wave of attacks on the working class is most likely on its way.

Eric Toussaint (Belgium) emphasised that there is no automatic link between the fact that the crisis is being paid for by workers and the popular masses, and an increase of social struggles. Political, ideological and organisational factors will also play a role in the development of the struggles.

Esther Vivas (Spain) and Daniel Tanuro (Belgium) brought in a fundamental analytical dimension with their introductions: the economic crisis cannot be observed in isolation from the global ecological and food crises. Vivas presented the causes and structure of the food crisis: the current model of agricultural and livestock production is in a large measure responsible for climate change. Tanuro demonstrated how the official, ruling class responses to climate change are insufficient, unreal, and irrational and put us in even more danger. He argued that eco-socialists should push for an end to unnecessary production, the retraining of workers in affected sectors and the development of a new agricultural model instigated by radical anti-capitalist measures.

Overall, the analyses revealed that the crisis is systemic, that those who are paying for it are the popular and working classes, and that now, more than ever, it is necessary to build an emancipatory, global anti-capitalist and eco-socialist project. IIRE is grateful for the coordinating resources which Bruno Jetin contributed.

Youth School

With 24 participants, 12 women and 12 men, coming from Denmark, Belgium, France, Philippines, Spain and Turkey, this year's IIRE Youth School proved a big success.

"This was a unique real experience in internationalism", said one of the young participants at the school which was tri-lingual with simultaneous interpretation between English, French and Spanish. The 10-day long IIRE Youth School provides young activists with a break from regular campaigning, creating a space where they come together to study and discuss more theoretical and strategic issues. The participants made good use of the Ernest Mandel Library, reading works of classical and contemporary radical thinkers.

Figure 21- IIRE Fellow Penelope Duggan and a youth school participant with co-director Bertil Videt and former co-director Antonio Carmona Báez

With a full day per topic, the participants had sufficient time to go in-depth with a number of challenges that progressive movements are faced with today.

This year we introduced a day on the economic crisis/es, in which IIRE Fellow Catherine Samary explained the current crisis as well as theoretical approaches to crises in capitalism.

Global Justice School

This year's annual Global Justice School, entitled Global Justice and the Capitalist Crisis took place from 28 November to 19 December. More than 25 participants from 16 different countries (Algeria, Colombia, Belgium, Benin, Euskadi, France, Italy, Lebanon, Mexico, Morocco, the Netherlands, Peru, the Philippines, Puerto Rico, Togo, and the United States) attended the School. Topics covered at this session included analyses of the current crisis from economic, gender, ethnic and ecological perspectives, in addition to regional experiences in Europe and Latin America and the questions linked to strategy and the building of national parties and an International. The participants brought in their different experiences, from trade-unionism to actions for the cancellation of debt and the defence of human rights.

This year, the School was divided into modules, allowing for those only able to attend one or two weeks instead of the full three, to do so while participating in a full coherent theme such as Economy, Climate Change and/or Political Strategies. For those who were not able to attend the whole three weeks, integration in the session was a bit more difficult, but on the whole, there was a real collective spirit and a good atmosphere.

The first module on the economic crisis, started with a two days course on a Marxist analysis of the world economy, its history of recurrent crises and the characteristics of the actual global responses to the crisis .This allowed the participants to use a common framework in looking at other aspects of the crisis (migration, identity politics, the new working class, imperialism, Latin America, the food crisis). The second module was new, in this module we tried to look again at Marx and productivism, at the climate crisis and at ecosocialism. The final module dwelt on more common grounds for revolutionaries and activists: how to build social movements, what are the links between social movements and parties, plan, market and democracy, to what extent is our vision of socialist democracy important in our daily work? The final session on why build an International, made a good synthesis of this module.

Participants came in a majority from non-European countries; the exchange between comrades from very different backgrounds was fertile and challenging. Questions like nationalism, religion, women's rights, came forward and provoked animated discussions in the evenings.

All participants expressed the wish to keep contact, amongst them and with the IIRE.

Public Activities

In line with its bi-annual work plan, IIRE in 2008 became known to wider circles of progressive forces, in Amsterdam and throughout Europe. IIRE is now a point of reference for public debate locally and it is the place where people come to hear and interact with internationally renowned guests of the radical left. More importantly, IIRE serves as a space for initiatives taken on by those activists who want to engage in collective learning in order to change the world.

Figure 22- Public events at the IIRE can attract a substantial audience

Returns of Marxism

In recent years we have seen a renewed interest in Marxism worldwide. A new generation is discovering the fertility of the many traditions of Marxism for understanding and attempting to change the world.

After a successful inaugural series of seminars in 2007/2008, Returns of Marxism continued in 2008/2009. Topics in this year lectures included: contemporary Latin American politics, the politics of gentrification, reading Capital, radical feminism, Marxism and philosophy and more. These seminar series aim to bring together scholars, writers and activists from different fields in order to discuss the relevance of Marxist ideas for contemporary debates.

As a sub-series of Returns of Marxism, 2009 offered a number of lectures under the heading Exploring Marx's Capital, linked to the Capital Reading Group organised by the IIRE (see below).

In the 2008-2009 academic year, Returns of Marxism, consisted of the following lectures (in chronological order):

○ The Left in Latin America - Lecture Series held by Jeff Webber, University of Toronto

○ Toward a Marxist Analysis of the Urban - Martin Cobian, University of Amsterdam

○ Storming Heaven: Autonomist Marxism, Workerism and the left today - Panel with: Steve Wright, Monash University Australia (author of 'Storming Heaven. Class composition and struggle in Italian Autonomist Marxism'), Katja Diefenbach, Jan van Eyck Akademie, Maastricht, Guglielmo Carchedi, University of Amsterdam, Peter Thomas, Historical Materialism and University of Amsterdam

○ Workers of the World: Essays toward a Global Labor History - Marcel van der Linden, International Institute of Social History, Amsterdam; Jurriaan Bendien, Archivist and Translator

○ Workers of the world, who washes your socks? Feminist critiques of Marxism in the late 1970s - Chiara Bonfiglioli, University of Utrecht

○ Exploring Marx's Capital: "The commodity and the form of value" - Peter Thomas, Historical Materialism and University of Amsterdam

○ The Cuban process: 1959-2009 - Antonio Carmona Báez, Executive Co-Director IIRE

○ Does Marx have a principle of distributive justice? - Wei Xiaoping, Philosophy Institute of Chinese Academy of Social Sciences

○ Is Marx a Fichtean? - Tom Rockmore, Philosophy Institute of Duquesne University of USA

○ Exploring Marx's Capital: The fetishism of commodities - Geert Reuten, University of Amsterdam

○ Exploring Marx's Capital: Money, the general formula of Capital and labour process - Riccardo Bellofiore, University of Bergamo

○ The national question in post Cold War Europe - Murray Smith, Former Co-Director IIRE

○ Exploring Marx's Capital: Constant and variable capital and surplus value - Guglielmo Carchedi, University of Amsterdam

○ Althusser and Marxist political analysis (the case of Yugoslavia) - Gal Kirm, Jan van Eyck Akademie, Maastricht

○ Exploring Marx's Capital: Relative surplus value, machinery and large-scale industry - Michael Kraetke, University of Amsterdam

○ Immigration in Europe today: Apartheid or civil cohabitation? - Darko Suvin, Professor Emeritus, McGill University

○ Exploring Marx's Capital: Absolute and relative surplus value and the accumulation of capital - Michael Heinrich, PROKLA - Zeitschrift fur kritische Sozialwissenschaft, Berlin

○ Contradictions and limits of neoliberal European governance - • Laura Horn, Vrije Universiteit Amsterdam

○ Exploring Marx's Capital: Primitive accumulation - Frieder Otto Wolf, Freie University, Berlin.

Capital Reading Group

Keeping up with the spirit of the times, the IIRE has been hosting two Das Kapital reading groups (English and Dutch) with the participation of international guest speakers lecturing in the Returns of Marxism series. Loaded with participatory assignments and collective discussion, the reading groups were well attended by a wide variety of activists, students and those interested in understanding the classical text. Both the Dutch and English language groups finalised the first of the three books of Karl Marx's most important work by the end of the year, and the English language group continues with the second book in 2010.

Palestine, Solidarity and the Left

Taking advantage of the high-level profile of those participating in the Palestine Seminar, IIRE -together with the Dutch bimonthly Grenzeloos, organised a public forum on Palestine on the16th of February. The evening started with clips from the documentary films 'Generation Intifada' and 'Welcome to Palestine' by radical film makers Chris Den Hond and Mireille Court. After this, Gilbert Achcar, IIRE fellow and Middle East expert, spoke about the international context of the latest war in Gaza. Sergio Yahni, of the Alternative Information Centre, offered a general summary of the political situation inside Israel and spoke specifically on the anti-war movement and the usefulness of boycotts and sanctions against the Israeli state. The final speaker was Lot van Baaren, a trade union and Palestine solidarity activist from Rotterdam, The Netherlands. She spoke about the prospects for the Dutch labour movement stepping up its solidarity with Palestine. The entire evening emphasized the important role grassroots solidarity can play in the search for alternatives. The audience was a mixed group of over sixty people consisting of mostly activists, students and local political figures of the Dutch left.

Europe Wide Meeting of Solidarity with Venezuela

On the weekend 19-21 June, the IIRE hosted the Europe-wide Meeting of Solidarity with the Bolivarian Republic of Venezuela. Over 120 people, representing diplomatic missions, Bolivarian Circles and other solidarity organisations from a wide field of activities, attended the three-day event co-sponsored by the Bolivarian Circle of The Netherlands and the Venezuelan Embassy at The Hague.

This historical meeting defined methodologies and practices for a diplomacy of the Peoples - and political education.

Figure 23- Attendees at the meeting of solidarity with the Bolivarian revolution

During the opening plenary session on Friday, IIRE Executive Co-Director Bertil Videt addressed the crowd with inspiring words of friendship, following a speech by the Venezuelan Ambassador to The Netherlands, Augustin Pérez Celis, who praised the Institute for its service to social activists and its solidarity with the Bolivarian Revolution. Together with three representatives of the Venezuelan Ministry of Foreign Affairs, Pérez Celis stressed the need for political education in their country as well as for the solidarity movements across Europe. The IIRE was identified as an important and strategically located progressive institution, a natural place to hold some educational sessions for Bolivarian and left activists in Europe.

Literature, Memory and Social Movements: Indonesia 2009

On July 1st, Australian freelance writer, translator and academic activist Max Lane delivered a talk on Literature, Memory and Social Movements in Indonesia at the IIRE. Lane's new book, Unfinished Nation: Indonesia Before and After Suharto (Verso Books, 2008), begins a discussion of the contradictions inherent in the processes that led to Suharto's overthrow. He is also known for his translation of the works of Indonesian dissident novelist Pramoedya Ananta Toer; among these: This Earth of Mankind (1996), Child of All Nations (1996) and Glass House (1997), all published by Penguin Books. Max Lane is currently a Fellow at the Department of Malay Studies, National University of Singapore.

Marx in Soho

On Friday, 3 July, Howard Zinn's Marx in Soho, was performed at the IIRE by the Vermont-based actor and Sociology professor Jerry Levy. The play, which is directed by Michael Fox Kennedy, depicts an imagined Return of Karl Marx to 21st Century New York. An icon of the American left, historian and activist Howard Zinn is most well known for his book A People's History of the United States.

The performance attracted a mixed audience, who engaged in a lively debate on the legacy and contemporary relevance of Karl Marx.

A Left View on the Neoliberal Crisis

In connection to the IIRE Economy Seminar (see above) the IIRE organised a public meeting on the economic crisis. By then, a year had past since the world fell into the deepest economic crisis since the 1930s and the end is nowhere in sight. Vulnerable groups like youth, migrants and precarious workers have been especially hard hit.

Still, many economists said that the crisis was ending. These were the same economists who, before the outbreak of the current mayhem, claimed it would never happen and they are the same ones who spent years encouraging the de-regularisation of the economy and privatisation of public services - part of the causes of the current crisis. In contrast, there are progressive economists who have always challenged neoliberal orthodoxy and who pointed out the dangers of the growing instability of the world economy.

In this context, the IIRE organised an evening with two internationally known critical economists and a Marxist theoretician on the 1st of October. IIRE Fellows and economists Michel Husson and Claudio Katz and with Chris Harman, the late editor of *International Socialism*, a Marxist theoretical journal published in Britain.

Staff and friends of the IIRE were saddened to hear about the sudden death of Chris Harman on the evening of 6 November.

Figure 24 - Grenzeloos editor Alex de Jong and Chris Harman (right) at a Dutch section of the Fourth International public meeting held at the IIRE

Publications

Ernest Mandel Biography: A Rebel's Dream Deferred

At last, the world can come to know the life of IIRE founder and Belgian revolutionary Marxist Ernest Mandel (1923-1995). The book written by Dutch biographer Jan Willem Stutje, the first who had unlimited access to Mandel's archives and notes is now available for purchase in its English translation.

One of the most prominent Marxist scholars of his time, Mandel made unsurpassable contributions to the economic analysis and to contemporary political thought for socialists of all tendencies. From surviving the Nazi concentration camps to Mandel's personal encounters with J.-P. Sartre, Che Guevara and Tariq Ali, author Jan Willem Stutje tells us the story of a human being who dedicated his life to democracy, socialism and worldwide revolution.

ISBN: 978-1844673162

Socialists and the Capitalist Recession

IIRE/Socialist Resistance, NSR no. 39/40 (216 pp.).

The 2008 credit crunch produced an international recession in 2009. In this new book Claudio Katz and Michel Husson, both fellows of the International Institute for Research and Education, and SSP activist Raphie de Santos lead an attempt not only to describe the present crisis, but also to understand its causes and debate socialist solutions. This 216-page book brings together much of the most powerful socialist analysis of the recession.

Sean Thompson shows how neoliberal globalisation has an in-built tendency towards deflation. As explained in the article by Francois Sabado, the period since the turn of the century has been a disaster for American capitalism; first the catastrophe in Iraq and of the Bush government in general, and now an economic collapse that has completely undermined the neoliberal 'Washington Consensus'.

The ideologues of capitalism are on the defensive. But the Marxist explanation of the crisis has to be hammered home. Who caused this crisis? Why did it occur? What is it in capitalism that leads to the globalisation of poverty while a tiny elite become mega-wealthy? And what are the possible alternatives? This book is a significant contribution to this debate.

The book also includes The Basic Ideas of Karl Marx, an outline by Ernest Mandel on the core ideas of scientific socialism.

IBSN: 978-0-902869-84-4

Strategies of Resistance

IIRE/Socialist Resistance, NSR no. 42/43 (182 pp.).

IIRE just published Strategies of Resistance & Who Are the Trotskyists?, a collection of works by IIRE Fellow Daniel Bensaïd including his history of Trotskyism, newly translated into English by Nathan Rao. This 182-page book has been published in cooperation with Resistance Books. The introduction by Paul Le Blanc gives a flavour of the contents:

"Daniel Bensaïd's challenging survey comes at an appropriate moment. It is a gift to activists reaching for some historical perspective that may provide hints as to where we might go from here. Embracing and sharing the revolutionary socialist political tradition associated with Leon Trotsky, Bensaïd is not simply a thoughtful radical academic or perceptive left-wing intellectual though he is certainly both but also one of the foremost leaders of an impressive network of activists, many of them seasoned by innumerable struggles."

ISBN: 978-0-902869-86-8

Newsletter

The electronic newsletter of the IIRE has become a main tool for informing our community about developments and activities at the IIRE. The distribution of the newsletter is now a regular monthly event, which keeps our friends up to date. The newsletter, originally in English only, became bi-lingual with a French translation from February 2009. In November 2009 a Spanish language version was added. By the end of 2009 the Newsletter had 1.284 subscribers.

Website

As more and more material is made available through the IIRE website the traffic increases. We observe a slow and steady increase in visits and hits to the www.iire.org website. In 2009 we had a daily average of 302 visits and 4350 hits.

The www.iiire.org website is updated frequently with news from IIRE fellows, news on IIRE activities and publications.

More sound files, in several languages, from our own seminars have been made available for the public, thanks to the IIRE podcast, at http://podcast.iire.org/.

The work of scanning older IIRE publications has been continued throughout 2009, and has made its first 21 English 'Notebooks for Study and Research' freely available as pdf files from the website.

A page for the IIRE is set up on Facebook, which had 730 fans by the end of the year[30], who get regular streams about IIRE activities to their Facebook account.

Library

Throughout 2009 the work in the library has been marked by the implementation of a new comprehensive and standardised library system, adopted in 2008. Most of the books of the library have, during 2009, been re-categorised in order to match the new categories.

So far the following new categories have been created:

IB working class & trade unions

ID youth & education

IE food production & consumption

IH (anti-) militarism & war

IJ globalisation & imperialism

IK social welfare & health

During each year, hundreds of books are donated to the IIRE library. The most used volumes added in 2009 include:

○ G. Achcar - Les Arabes et la Shoah

○ H. Belallouf - Grand Moyen Orient: Guerres ou paix? Plaidoyer pour une nouvelle révolution Arabe

○ Besancenot, (dialoga con Flavia D'Angeli) -La nostra sinistra.

○ Bloco de Esquerda - 51 ideias para mudar Portugal

○ D. Chavez, P. Barrett & C. Rodriguez Garavito - Utopia Reborn: The New Latin American Left

○ Hugo Chavez presents Simon Bolivar - The Bolivarian Revolution

○ L. Colletti - From Rousseau to Lenin

○ G. Frank - ReOrient: global economy in the Asian age

○ R. Kersten & D. Williams (eds.) - The Left in the Shaping of Japanese Democracy

○ K. Landais - Passions militantes et rigueur historienne vol.1 & 2

○ M. Majid - Les Luttes de Classes au Maroc depuis l'Independance

○ M. R. Mencherini - Guerre froide, gruerres rouges. Parti Communiste, stalinisme et luttes sociales en France. Les guerres insurrectionnelles de 1947-1948

30   This number had risen to 1,200 by October 2010.

- M. Mikula (ed.) - Women, Activism and Social Change
- Negri & F. Guattari - Communists like us
- Negri & M. Hardt - Empire
- Negri & M. Hardt - Multitude
- Neuberg - Armed Insurrection
- T. Oishi - The Unknown Marx. Reconstructing a Unified Perspective
- H. Patomoi - Democratising Globalisation. The Leverage of the Tobin Tax
- Red Notes - Working Class Autonomy and the Crisis. Italian Marxist Texts of Theory and Practice of a Class Movement, 1964-1979
- Semiotext(e) -Italy: Autonomia. Post-political politics
- D. Sogge - Give & Take. What's the matter with foreign aid?
- K. Theweleit - Male Fantasies vol. 1: Women, Floods, Bodies, History
- E. Toussaint - La Crise, quelles crises?
- J. Wallach Scott - Feminism and History
- S. Zizek - Violence

Research and Fellowship

In March 2008, the Amsterdam-branch of the (Dutch) Socialist Party, together with the radical alternative-green political group Amsterdam Anders-De Groene donated the money and resources to kick off a research project to define a progressive vision for the City of Amsterdam. The participatory research project consisted of 5 public meetings, where experts were invited to talk on such essential aspects as global finance and grand urban projects, transportation and infrastructure, housing and diversity, energy and participatory democracy. The debates were documented (in Dutch) and served as the basis for the two political groups to build a concrete platform for the 2010 municipal elections. Thanks to kind donations and to the (Dutch) Foundation for Research and Scientific Socialism (SOWS), two part-time coordinators were employed specifically for this project; namely, Martin Cobian (Puerto Rico) a PhD candidate at the City University of New York and Linda Coenen, a long time community organiser and activist from the Amsterdam squatter movement.

Fellow Highlights

Gilbert Achcar

On its 60th anniversary, the Zionist state made a last effort to decimate the vestiges of Palestinian resistance in Gaza by massively bombing the already frail infrastructure of schools, hospitals and government buildings, in addition to killing of thousands of people. Gilbert Achcar, also professor of International Relations at the University of London School of Oriental and Asian Studies, began this year writing extensively on the massacre and was interviewed by alternative as well as mainstream media internationally. In February, IIRE held its first international seminar on Palestine. Achcar's contribution to seminar was of the utmost importance. Together with IIRE Fellow Noam Chomsky, Achcar produced a second and augmented edition of the book Perilous Power: The Middle East and US Foreign Policy-Dialogues on Terror, Democracy, War and Justice Paradigm Publishers, Boulder/London

Daniel Bensaïd

As our report went to press, the international radical left lost one of its greatest intellectual authors. During the last year of his life, Daniel Bensaïd produced a number of essays articulating a Marxist line on the cluster of crises that the world is currently facing. His works and militancy were essential to the building of France's New Anti-capitalist Party. His last works were The Powers of Communism, published in Contretemps, where Bensaïd served as editor and a special working paper for IIRE Productivism and Ecology, an epistemological work on the topic of environment, capital and labour.

Claudio Katz

In Argentina, University of Buenos Aires professor of economy Claudio Katz spent most of his time publishing on the nature and effects of the current global financial crisis. This year, many of his works were translated into English and French from Spanish. He continues to participate in a regional dialogue of Marxist economists that promote the radical transformation of society through the taking of power by workers. His participation at the IIRE Economy Seminar in October was indispensible, as he brought an essentially Latin American perspective to a Northern-dominated debate.

Stephanie Coontz

Few academic works on the contemporary family have emanated from the left. But Stephanie Coontz continues to be an exception to the rule. This year, Coontz, who teaches at Evergreen State College in Olympia, Washington, published a second and expanded edition of the textbook American Families: A Multicultural Reader. Stephanie Coontz carries on teaching on history, gender and cultural diversity.

James Cockcroft

In April, IIRE Fellow and award winning author James Cockcroft spoke on The US Presidential Election and Escalating Intervention in Latin America at Las Jornadas Bolivarianas, held at the Federal University at Florianopolis (Santa Catarina), Brazil. In November, Cockcroft toured Cuba after attending the fourth International Colloquium of the Cuban Institute for Friendships among Peoples. He remains active in campaigning for the liberation of Cuban five, illegally detained in the United States.

Peter Drucker

In 2008, former IIRE co-director Peter Drucker played a cornerstone role in the organising of two major events for IIRE. First, the Palestinian Seminar held in February and second was the Institute's fourth international LGBT Seminar held in July. Drucker continues to serve on the editorial board of the Dutch socialist-alternative magazine *Grenzeloos* and publishes regularly on issues of sexuality and ethnicity. While employed as a professional translator, Peter Drucker keeps up his voluntary commitment to IIRE by lecturing at all our educational sessions.

Penelope Duggan

While serving on the Bureau and at the Secretariat of the Fourth International in Paris, Penelope Duggan maintains her militancy locally in the newly founded French New Anti-capitalist Party, as well as working closely with the permanent staff of IIRE in Amsterdam. This year, Penelope played a crucial role in organising the international Women's Seminar, which was successfully held in July and the Lecturer's Seminar held in April. She regularly lectures at all IIRE educational sessions. In February this year, Duggan spoke on Helena Molony (1884-1967) at the symposium "Irish Socialist Lives", organised by the Irish Labour History Society at the National University in Galway, Ireland.

Eric Toussaint

While continuing to advise the progressive governments of Bolivia, Ecuador, Paraguay and Venezuela, IIRE Fellow Eric Toussaint also serves the global justice movement with his knowledge of economic policies and their socio-political consequences. Toussaint continues to lead the CADTM International Debt Observatory, which – this year – held various conferences and training sessions on the effects of the current financial crisis, as well as on the growing food crisis in the Global South. Toussaint presence at the World Social Forum, held in Belem, Brazil, was essential in the drafting of the Declaration of the Assembly of Social Movements; which, for the first time, called for the building of a feminist, anti-capitalist and eco-socialist movement to radically transform our world. Toussaint also participated in the international Economy Seminar held in September.

Marcel van der Linden

After the publication of his groundbreaking Workers of the World Unite: Essays towards a Global History of Labour at the end of 2008, Marcel van der Linden continued to publish on Marxism, the international labour movement and the anti-capitalist movement globally. This year he co-edited four volumes in English and German with Prabhu Mohapatra, Karl Heinz Roth, Max Henninger, Angelika Ebbinghaus, Magaly Rofriguez García, Jasmien van Daele and Geert van Goethem. Van der Linden still serves as the Director of Research for the Amsterdam-based International Institute of Social History.

Michel Husson

Just like for many IIRE Fellows, the global financial meltdown of 2008-2009 kept Michel Husson busy analysing and writing on the inherent contradictions of contemporary capitalism. This year, Husson wrote numerous articles, which have been translated into English, on the nature of the current crisis and has engaged in public debate with such diverse figures of the international left like Chris Harman. He continues to work at the Paris-based Institute for Economic and Social Research (IRES).

Pierre Rousset

Pierre Rousset continues to be a leading figure in the Fourth International. He writes prolifically on the anti-capitalist movement in

Europe and Asia, and occasionally on the World Social Forum process. This year proved to be important for the international left in Asia, as many countries saw the rising and radicalisation of workers in China, Korea and Indonesia. Rousset documented the tragic political violence that the Sri Lankan government committed against the Tamil people, new political developments in Pakistan and the work of solidarity in Mindanao, Philippines. Pierre Rousset coordinates the website information centre Europe Solidaire san Frontieres (ESSF).

Our Fellows in 2009

Gilbert Achcar (France/Lebanon), Daniel Bensaïd (France), Susan Caldwell (Canada), Noam Chomsky (USA), James Cockcroft (Canada), Stephanie Coontz (USA), Peter Drucker (USA / Netherlands), Penelope Duggan (Britain / France), Eva Ferraren (Philippines / Netherlands), Janette Habel (France), Michel Husson (France), Claudio Katz (Argentina), Marcel van der Linden (Netherlands), Michael Löwy (Brazil/France), David Mandel (Canada), Braulio Moro (Mexico), Pierre Rousset (France), Catherine Samary (France), Anthony Arthur Smith (USA), Eric Toussaint (Belgium), Josette Trat (France), Francois Vercammen (Belgium), Peter Waterman (Netherlands/UK).

Organisation

IIRE General Assembly

The IIRE Association, our governing body, held its annual General Assembly from 21 to 22 February. The group approved the 2008 Annual Report, as well as the 2009 Budget and Work Plan. The General Assembly expressed great satisfaction with the results achieved over the last year, and applauded the ambitious work plan, which included: the production of international publications, three activist seminars, an IIRE fund drive, a Global Justice School, a Youth School and digitalisation of our library catalogue.

Lecturers' Seminar

On Saturday, April 25th, IIRE Fellows and selected friends who often lecture at IIRE educational sessions met to discuss the format and content of future programmes. With an introductory talk by Francois Sabado on the nature of the current global financial and ecological crises, participants were motivated to restructure the school format and modify its content. Special attention was given to climate change and the eco-socialist debate, the effects of the global financial crisis and how it impacts the working class in all its diversity. Executive co-directors Bertil Videt and Antonio Carmona Báez addressed the fellows with evaluations of previous schools and methodological considerations in the spirit of Brazilian Marxist pedagogue Paolo Freire. Considering the reality of working Europeans, who might not be able to take an entire three-weeks off for the Global Justice School, the format of working in week-long modules was adopted.

A clear result of this meeting was the reorganisation of this year's Global Justice School, which was centred on three modules (see above).

Staff

In September the IIRE bade farewell to Antonio Carmona Báez, who had served as Executive Co- Director since April 2008. Antonio has taken up a teaching position in International Relations at the University of Amsterdam. As a member of the IIRE Executive Board, he will continue to serve the Institute on a voluntary basis.

The IIRE welcomes its new Executive Co-Director, Marijke Colle. Originally from Ghent, Belgium, Marijke Colle has been a social activist since the European student and workers uprisings of 1968. Her history of activism includes but is not limited to feminist struggles, the defence of reproductive rights, the trade union movement, environmental politics and the organisation of youth, and she has been a friend and volunteer at the Institute since its foundation in 1982.

Since February 2009 Aat van Wijk is working, on a freelance basis, with the commercial activities of the IIRE. Aat van Wijk assists Financial and Administrative Manager Eng Que with developing and implementing marketing strategies, as well as receiving commercial clients.

IIRE Manila

The idea to establish an IIRE in Manila, the Philippine capital, started about two years ago. Realising such an important project was very challenging for the Philippine partners, especially logistically and financially. In order to systematically realise the project, an IIRE-Manila Team composed of activists-volunteers was organised and key persons were deployed from the Southern island of Mindanao to Manila.

The first focus of the IIRE-Manila team was resource generation, physical set-up of the institute and network building in the National Capital Region. With the help of international and local networks and friends, the IIRE Manila was able to modestly sustain its operation and slowly build-up the physical infrastructure of the institute by acquiring needed fixtures and resource materials. The institute was also able to connect with some key and strategic networks and personalities ranging from different political blocks, movements and Non-Government Organizations in Manila. The IIRE-Manila was able to join meetings, discussions and mobilisations in Manila during this period.

Presently, the IIRE-Manila has already a relatively equipped office and already in touch with some strategic networks and partners in Manila, and even in a few Asian countries. Initiatives are now directed towards preparing for the next school, while at the same time continuing resource generation works in order to sustain its operations and to fully establish its library and resource materials. Activities and initiatives that would foster stronger ties with the established networks in Manila are presently being developed. Among others, these initiatives include the following: monthly group discussions on various issues among second-line activists of the broad left, a periodic Lecture Series on Mindanao Concerns aiming towards organising a network of Mindanaoans in Manila, and some initiatives dealing with internal and external migration in the country.

Finances and Commercial activities

Since its relaunch mid-2007 IIRE pursues a strategy of commercial letting of meeting rooms and bedrooms in order to ensure a continuous income.

Comparing our performance in 2008 with 2009, we see a big increase in the turnover of meeting rooms. This can be explained by 1) the marketing campaign in beginning 2008, 2) brand recognition, 3) word of mouth and 4) networking. The letting of bedrooms remained stable and the slight decrease in turnover from extras can be explained by less requests for lunches and receptions during or after meetings.

It is only thanks to generous donations from our supporters that the two Global Justice Schools, in Amsterdam and Manila, have been realised. The IIRE still depends on donations in order to pursue its educational programme.

How you can help.
Antonio Carmona Báez

The IIRE is an active institute, which is proud of its achievements. We want to expand our activities, which we feel are badly needed in the present world situation. We invite everybody who agrees with our aims to help us with the further development of our project, financially or through other forms. Founded in Belgium, we were officially recognized as an international scientific foundation by a Royal Decree of 11 June 1981. Contributions to our work are tax-deductible in several countries, for example in the US through the Centre for Changes International Fund.

Figure 25- The IIRE is a unique meeting place

Compared to other similar institutions, we carry out our work with an absurdly low budget. We receive no government subsidies. No money is spent on high staff salaries, public relations or luxurious meals or accommodations for participants. Everything is done with a minimal staff, with unpaid international Fellows and volunteers who often pay all or part of their fares to and from Amsterdam, and with the labour contributed by the participants themselves. We could not have launched and maintained the IIRE without the help of many people: not just donors, but the many volunteers who have come from several countries to help with painting, repairs, and electrical work.

We are also grateful to the friends who have left their libraries to us in their wills; and particularly our lecturers, translators and interpreters, many of whom wholly or partly donate their services. This multi-faceted help will be as essential in the next century as it has been in our first two decades. If you can help in any of these ways, please contact us. Despite these contributions, the Institute costs money. We need money for plane fares: plane fares from the Third World must more and more often be completely covered by the Institute. We need money for our building, which though beautiful is old. We have carried out major renovations and improvements in recent years, but more are needed....

We also need money for food (although participants cook for themselves during their stays). We need money for gas, water, light, heat, property taxes, photocopying, phone calls.... In recent years we have benefited from the support of Germany's Jakob Moneta Stiftung, Canada's Kimeta Society and Sweden's Tom Gustafsson Memorial Fund, as well as from generous legacies in one or two wills. But regular, annual, individual donations remain crucial to our survival. We confront simultaneously a rise in costs and a struggle to find new donations. We are doing our part to breathe new life into hope and faith in the future. But we can only do it with new sources of financial support: we must acquire new donors if the Institute is to maintain and expand its work. We rely on your help.

IIRE has signed a contract with the Dutch Foundation for Research and Education in Scientific Socialism (SOWS). The SOWS has decided to support the political and educational activities held at the Institute. Such activities include Youth, Women, Middle East, LGBTT and Climate Change Schools and Seminars, plus IIRE publications. In return IIRE will ask it supporters to become a donor for SOWS. SOWS will use these funds exclusively for IIRE but decides on a yearly basis which activities of IIRE will be supported. We encourage our readers to consider testament pledges and other donations. Suggested regular donations from IIRE friends are 25, 50 and 100 euros, but any donation will of course be appreciated.

Notebooks for Study and Research

19/20	The Fragmentation of Yugoslavia: An Overview, Catherine Samary	(60 pp. €5)
21	Factory Commitees and Workers' Control in Petrograd in 1917, David Mandel	(48 pp. €5)
22	Women's Lives in the New Global Economy, Penelope Duggan & Heather Dashner (editors)	(68 pp. € 5)
23	Lean Production: Capitalist Utopia? Tony Smith	(68 pp. €5)
24/25	World Bank/IMF/WTO: The Free-Market Fiasco, Susan George, Michel Chossudovsky et al.	Out of print
26	The Trade-Union Left and the Birth of a New South Africa, Claude Jacquin	(92 pp., €5)
27/28	Fatherland or Mother Earth? Essays on the National Question , Michael Löwy	(108 pp., €16, £10.99, $16)
29/30	Understanding the Nazi Genocide: Marxism after Auschwitz, Enzo Traverso	(154 pp., €19.20, £13, $19.)
31/32	Globalization: Neoliberal Challenge, Radical Responses, Robert Went	(170 pp., €21, £14, $21)
33/34	The Clash of Barbarisms: September 11 & the Making of the New World Disorder, Gilbert Achcar	(128 pp., €15, £10, $16)
35/36	The Porto Alegre Alternative: Direct Democracy in Action, Iain Bruce ed.	(162 pp., €19, £13, $23.50)
37/38	Take the Power to Change the World, Phil Hearse ed.	(144 pp., €9, £6, $12)
39/40	Socialists and the Capitalist Recession (with Ernest Mandel's 'Basic Theories of Karl Marx') Raphie De Santos, Michel Husson, Claudio Katz	(196 pp., €9, £7, $12)
41	Living our Internationalism: The IIRE's history, Murray Smith and Joost Kircz eds.	(104 pp, €5, £4, $7)

42/43	Strategies of Resistance & 'Who Are the Trotskyists' Daniel Bensaïd	(196 pp. €8, £6, $10)
44/45	Building Unity Against Fascism: Classic Marxist Writings, Leon Trotsky, Daniel Guérin, Ted Grant	(164 pp., €8, £6, $10)
46	October Readings: The development of the concept of Permanent Revolution, D. R. O'Connor Lysaght ed.	(110pp, €5)
47	The Long March of the Trotskyists: A contribution to the history of the International, Pierre Frank	(168 pp €8, £6, $10)
48	Women Liberation & Socialist Revolution: Documents of the Fourth International, Penelope Duggan ed.	(194 pp €8, £6, $10)

Forthcoming

- Dangerous relationships, Marriage and divorces between Marxism and feminism, Cinzia Arruzza
- Marxism and Anarchism, Marx, Lenin, Trotsky et al.
- New Left Parties: Experiences from Europe, Bertil Videt et al.
- Returns of Marxism, Sara Farris and Antonio Carmona Báez eds.
- Revolution and Counter-revolution in Europe, Pierre Frank
- The conflict in Palestine, Cinzia Nachira ed.
- Women and the Crisis, Terry Conway ed.

Subscribe online at: http://bit.ly/NSRsub

To order, email iire@iire.org or write to International Institute for Research and Education, Lombokstraat 40, NL-1094, Amsterdam.

www.ingramcontent.com/pod-product-compliance
Lightning Source LLC
Chambersburg PA
CBHW021836020426
42334CB00014B/660